DIVORCE & REMARRIAGE

made beautiful in His time!

One Christian's
experience of
Divorce
&
Remarriage

Don E. Cunningham

TATE PUBLISHING & *Enterprises*

TATE PUBLISHING
& Enterprises

Divorce & Remarrriage Made Beautiful in His Time
Copyright © 2006 by Don E. Cunningham. All rights reserved.
Visit www.tatepublishing.com for more information.

Scripture quotations are taken from The New King James Version /
Thomas Nelson Publishers, Nashville: Thomas Nelson Publishers. Copyright © 1982. Used by permission. All rights reserved.

All of the individuals referred to in this book are real. To protect the
identity of most of them, the author has changed their names. Actual
names are used only where written permission has been granted by the
people identified in the book. The author thanks them for this and for the
blessings they have contributed to his life.

Cover design by Melanie Harr-Hughes
Interior design by Liz Mason

Published in the United States of America

ISBN: 1-5988654-8-X
07.07.06

DIVORCE & REMARRIAGE
made beautiful in His time!

is dedicated to

my loving wife, Sharon, who over the past twenty-five years has exemplified the love of Christ in our relationship. She has been the willing instrument our Savior and Lord has used to make all things beautiful in our marriage.

Acknowledgements

I would like to recognize those who have touched my life in positive ways throughout my divorce and remarriage. Some are recognized within the pages of this book; for others I have used fictitious names. I wish to express my heartfelt thanks to Ron and Wilna Heeks, Dr. Samuel McDill, Ron and Maggie Thompson, and other fellow-workers at Tri Counties Regional Center. I am especially indebted to Maggie, who spent hours critiquing my manuscript and writing the foreword to my book. I am indebted to Rev. Terry Reid, who reopened the door to a pastoral care and outreach ministry for me. I appreciate the members of our Single Persons in Christian Endeavors (SPICE), who were fellow travelers along the pathway of divorce.

I am thankful for Elaine Hardt, the leader of our Christian Writers Group. Her insights, encouragement, and gentle guidance have influenced the structure and readability of this book. The members of our group have been a weekly inspiration.

A thank you also goes to Kay Strahm, who started me on the path of writing this book over twenty years ago. She laid a solid foundation on which to build. A special thank you to Kathy Parker, M.A., who has helped encourage us along the path of aging.

To my niece, Nancy Riddell, who after a brief discussion told me, "Uncle Don, you should write a book about divorce and remarriage." It was her comment that led me to refocus on its completion.

I am especially grateful to my wife, Sharon, who has made the reality of God's love a day-by-day experience. Our Lord made my divorce beautiful through His healing, loving Spirit and support of true friends. Through Sharon, He daily demonstrates that remarriage is an especially beautiful experience.

My prayer for those of you who are walking through the valley of the shadow of divorce is that this book, God's Word, Christian counseling and fellowship with other Christians walking the same path will support you as you move toward finding that divorce can be made beautiful in His time.

Hugs, In Christ's and My Love,
Don E. Cunningham

Table of Contents

Introduction	11
1. A Marriage Doomed to Failure	13
2. Pointing Fingers and Helping Hands	33
3. The Walking "Corpse" of Divorce	43
4. Weekend Visit to the Love Cave	51
5. Lonely Apartment Dweller to Back Bedroom Grandpa	55
6. The Shattered Platter	65
7. Forgiving Those Who Trespass Against Us	75
8. Welcome to the Lord's Table	79
9. Does Jesus Really Understand?	87
10. Bound by a Band	93
11. To Remain Single or Remarry – That Is the Question	97
12. Behold My Special Princess!	103
13. An Unusual Proposal and a Delayed Response	115
14. Wedding Bells Ring	129
15. You Mean I Can't Lead, Lord—or Can I?	141
16. Remarriage Beautiful All the Time!	149
17. We Plan For the Future	163
Appendix A – Scripture for: "Divorce's Depression – Forgiveness' Delight"	179
Appendix B – A Short Story: "Mara"	185
Appendix C – Scripture for: "Divorce and God's Grace"	193
Bibliography	199

Foreword

Don Cunningham is all about being a Christian gentleman, a man of faith. He has lived his life with a high degree of compassion. Working in the field of social services, as a pastor and teacher, he has been a responsive friend to many. Having known Don for thirty years, I realized after reading this book how accurately it reflects his integrity. When Don found himself in a loveless marriage, he began a painstaking search through prayer, study of Scripture, and counseling to discern the path Christ meant for him. In a society where divorce is now a common experience, it is heartening to witness the depth of Don's self-questioning. He grapples with the many considerations of divorce and remarriage in a fundamentalist faith tradition that too often burdens its followers with shame. This is an honest, intimate account of Don's faith journey. The study Don has put forth will ease the way and provide hope for other Christians facing divorce. Included is the possibility of celebrating the joy of remarriage. Don writes with a fresh sincerity, his unique brand of humor, and above all, an indomitable spirit of Christian love.

Maggie Shopen Thompson
Calais, Vermont
February, 2006

INTRODUCTION

Several years ago, during her lecture on death and dying, Dr. Elisabeth Kubler-Ross was asked, "How do you explain anything as horrible as death to a child?"

Dr. Kubler-Ross responded, "With that attitude, you don't."

Those in the early, traumatic stages of divorce may be struggling with a very similar question. "How am I going to get through the horrible death of a relationship?"

This book speaks to that question. Walk with me through the valley of the shadow of divorce into the rich assurance that He makes even divorce beautiful in His time. Learn what many of us have experienced as we traveled down that lonely, guilt-ridden path. It is a path that can lead to depression and defeat, or to the exhilarating challenge of growth and victory.

Observe how I struggled within a failing marriage, and note the counseling attempts to save it. See how internal and external pressures moved it towards its death, and see the ensuing despair and depression of separation and divorce. As a Christian, I had to face the spiritual issues of divorce and remarriage. A psalm of despair and a poem of divorce are intended to illustrate the initial depression through which I walked.

A song in the night changed the direction of my heart from despair to hope. It placed divorce within a Christian perspective, leading to healing through Scripture and Christian counseling. The forgiveness of my sins of divorce and the psychological healing of temperament became very clear through a psychological testing instrument and interaction with those around me. The Lord brought fresh meaning to Scripture and guided me through various aspects of my relationship with friends, the church body, and my precious loving Savior. He put my shattered platter back together, bringing healing and forgiveness.

Poems move from despair to hope. The shadows in the valley fade as my understanding of the light of His presence becomes clearer.

As the healing takes place, a new question must be faced. "Is it possible for a Christian to remarry?" The question soon changes to, "How can I best serve my Lord?"

During a long period of prayer, the answer comes, and I address the question, "What do I have to offer to a woman?" Once resolved, I look at what kind of lady would best match my temperament and personality. The blueprint is presented to our Lord in prayer.

A new lady comes into my life in Sunday school. The remainder of the book looks at our courtship, engagement, wedding, and twenty-five years of a wonderful relationship. The Lord improved on my blueprint and gave me Sharon.

Our wedding verse was, "He makes all things beautiful in His time."

Poetry, from the time of our first date and throughout our marriage, portrays the beauty of a relationship made in Sunday school and designed in Heaven. Yes, He makes even divorce and remarriage beautiful in His time!

The final chapter of this book looks at our planning for the future and deals with the responsibilities that older partners have toward their younger spouses. In reality, it presents issues that should be carefully considered by all who enter into that mystifying relationship between husband and wife.

Friend, wherever you are in your journey through the valley of the shadow of divorce, I hope this book will guide you toward the point where in joy you can exclaim, "He makes even divorce beautiful in His time!" Perhaps you may eventually rejoice in the beautiful experience of remarriage.

Chapter 1
A Marriage Doomed to Failure

The Drunken Divorced Sailor

In late August, 1955, on a hot, humid night, I drove from Providence, Rhode Island, to Maria's family home in upstate New York. I stopped at a red light in a small town in Massachusetts. A staggering, drunken sailor leaned through my car window and asked for a ride. I asked him where he was going, and he replied, "Albany." I told him to hop in and off we went.

As we drove toward Troy, he told me his name was Roy and that he was stationed out of Boston. He dozed off for a while. When he awoke, I stopped at a coffee shop. We talked as we drank a couple of cups of coffee and then headed once again toward our destination.

Roy began talking about his three failed marriages. He said his latest wife kicked him out when he arrived home drunk, so he decided to spend his shore leave with his parents. He asked what I did for a living. I told him I attended Bible college and worked as a janitor to meet my family's needs. When he learned I was preparing to become a minister, he began a tirade about how he believed in God, but now he hated Him because He didn't save any of his three marriages. God just didn't care what happened to him.

I listened to him as he related all the things that went wrong in each of his marriages. He got very specific about how each wife didn't understand him; how much they argued with him about his drinking; how sometimes it turned into an out-and-out brawl. He finally asked me, "Now do you see why I hate God?"

I pulled over to the side of the road, looked him in the eyes, and said, "NO."

Shocked, he angrily responded, "What do you mean, 'NO'?"

"I have listened to you half way across Massachusetts while you have talked about all of the problems you had throughout your three failed marriages. Not once did you mention any attempt to involve God or to follow the teaching of His word regarding your marriages. At what point in your dating did you ask Him to reveal to your heart if this was the right woman for you? When did you show your wife the love outlined in I Corinthians thirteen? Certainly in your arguments and fighting you weren't expressing love or giving your life for her as Christ did for the church. Yet you say God is to blame for not saving your marriages. No, I don't agree."

While I spoke with Roy, his anger turned to reflection, then to remorse, and then to tears. As we chatted, Roy accepted Christ into his heart. He vowed he would win back his third wife by reading and following God's teachings about marriage.

When we arrived in Troy, I stopped at my favorite hot dog stand on Congress Street. Roy and I chatted while we ate. When we finished, I took him to the bus stop where he could catch his bus to Albany. We prayed together as we waited for his bus. I gave him my address but never heard from him again.

Through the years, I have found that Roy's feelings are echoed over and over again in divorced people's lives. They blame God for their failures, even though they never fully involve Him in their marriages.

Marriage Is for Life

In my own Christian experience I was taught both by word and example that Christians don't get divorced. Our Lord hates divorce. When you marry, it is until death do you part. Divorce is not an option for the Christian. Over hundreds of years Bibli-

cal scholars have shown from God's Word that divorce is only permissible in the case of a spouse's fornication. While in such an instance divorce is permissible, it is not mandatory.

In their book, *Meant to Last*, Steele and Ryrie outline and critique the five different views regarding divorce. They are: Patristic view – divorce allowable in the case of adultery, but remarriage never permitted; Erasmian view – allowed for divorce and remarriage of the innocent party (most popular among evangelicals); Preteritive view – Christ bypassed the exception clause—for adultery—thus holding to the original intent of marriage with no divorce; Betrothal view – engaged but having "porneia" (premarital un-chastity) is a cause for divorce: and Consanguity view – an unlawful marriage-sexual incest was a cause for divorce, but remarriage was not permitted. This is the view held by the authors. For detailed discussion of these views, see *Meant to Last,* pages 99 – 117. They make the strong point that all five views agree that monogamy is God's best plan, and that divorce under God's law is a concession made due to hardened hearts.

They also note that only the Erasmian view allows for remarriage. They conclude that a divorced person should either reconcile to his spouse or remain unmarried.[1]

Why then, with so much evidence that divorce and remarriage are not an option for the Christian, did I become divorced and remarried? There was never any infidelity on the part of Maria or me. Instead of thirty years of endearing ourselves to each other, why did we find ourselves tragically enduring one another? It was clear that our hearts had become hardened in our relationship. Where did it all begin?

Greenhorn on the Dating Scene, and Runt in the Guard

During my high school years, I worked after school and weekends. I never had time to date, but I occasionally went to a Saturday night dance. On a couple of those occasions, I walked young ladies home. After graduation, on Saturday evenings my brother, Moe, cousin Eugene and I went to square dances. The year following graduation, a friend, John, asked me if I would take his sister to her senior prom. Lois was a very soft-spoken, gentle young lady with soft blue eyes, a pleasant smile, and golden tresses. She was always nearby when her brother and I sat and talked about our soccer games. I asked her if I could take her to her senior prom. She shyly responded, "Yes."

When I arrived at Lois's home, her dad met me at the door and told me I was the only one of his son's friends he trusted. He expected us home by midnight. Throughout the evening, we had fun dancing, talking, and laughing. We headed home slightly before her curfew. By the time I dropped off the other couple who had ridden with us, we arrived at her front door about five minutes past midnight. We were met on the front porch by her father and mother. He expressed concern that we weren't home on time, but said he still trusted me. They then asked if we enjoyed the prom. We both responded, "Yes." While Lois and I enjoyed the evening together, it would be our first and last date. A short time later, a new girl would enter my life. I did, however, maintain my friendship with John and was always warmly greeted by the family. I failed to recognize that they, like my family, were strong, supportive, and loving. I often wonder what my marital destiny would have been if we had continued dating. At twenty, I was a very inexperienced, socially naïve young man.

I met Maria while visiting my cousin Eugene in the hospital. His left arm was severely mutilated while he was doing maintenance work on a large box-corrugating machine. Part of his hair was pulled out before he was able to hit the emergency stop button. Shortly after I arrived at his room, his red-haired, freckled-faced wife, Michelle, came in with her cute blonde sister, Maria. We struck up a conversation and began kidding with one another.

When I prepared to leave, Maria told her sister she was going to take the bus home. I didn't have a car at the time, so I offered to accompany her to the bus stop. While walking on the icy sidewalk she slipped and fell. She wasn't injured, but I

insisted on riding home with her on the bus. When we arrived at her bus stop, I took her arm and walked with her up the hill to her house. The icy slush crunched beneath our feet.

As we entered the driveway, her mother heard our laughter, opened the door, and invited me in for a cup of coffee. While I had never drunk coffee before, I accepted her invitation. We sat around the kitchen table and chatted. Her mother was a soft-spoken lady with a pleasant smile. I became so engrossed in our conversation that I lost track of time. I missed the last bus and walked the five miles home. The snow resumed its downward flight, and a crisp breeze whisked it around me. The icy slush crunched in rhythm with my steps. One chilled-to-the-bone, lighthearted young man crept quietly through the front door, undressed and slipped exhausted into bed.

The following day I phoned Maria and invited her to go to a movie. She accepted! Our dates formed a pattern: visits at the hospital, movies, hamburgers at the Fifth Avenue Diner, ice cream sundaes at Tully's Ice Cream Parlor, bus rides, coffee at her mom's kitchen table, and my long walks home alone. We spent many Saturday nights eating pizza and dancing at a little Italian, family-run pizzeria. Occasionally, we went on dates and picnics with her friends.

Even though we seldom kissed and were never intimate, I was head-over-heels in love with her. She was reluctant to consider marrying me. Then, almost simultaneously, two unexpected events happened. The first one occurred when she had an argument with her father, dropped out of high school in her senior year, and went to live with her married sister, Michelle.

The second event happened when her brother, Ralph, and I went on field training at Pine Camp (Fort Drum) in northern New York. We both were in the 27th Infantry Division, 105th Regiment of the New York National Guard. He was in B Company from Cohoes, and I was in C Company from Troy. The first Sunday of our encampment, I went over to his barracks to see him. Shortly after my arrival, a burly looking, six-foot-two fellow began making very lewd remarks about him and his sisters. I told him to knock it off—that I was dating Maria. He made some more crude sexual remarks about her. I jumped over a bunk and hit him in the midsection with all my 128 pounds. The force drove him against the barrack clapboards, which gave way to his over 200 pound frame. I continued pounding on him until some of his barrack buddies pulled me away. The fellow staggered to his feet and apologized. I told him he better stop his abusive language toward Ralph and his sisters. He told me he would. We shook hands, and I returned to my barracks.

A few minutes later, the first sergeant from B Company confronted my first sergeant. I was not to come over to their barracks again. He was having the few loose boards nailed back into place. He went on to say that he could not have a runt company clerk beating up the toughest guy in his company. It was not good for morale. They both had a beer and a hardy laugh. They fought together in the South Pacific and were close friends. Of course, that brought an end to my visits to Company B and Ralph.

Upon our return home, Ralph told Maria about the incident. A short time later, she decided to accept my proposal. Looking back, I believe my defense of her, which grew out of my strong convictions of respect for women—especially my mother, sister, and Maria—lead to her decision to marry me.

On Sunday mornings I continued to teach my young boys' class and attend church. I spent afternoons visiting with her and her family. One Sunday evening I invited her to attend a special service we were having. My class was to present a skit about the fields being white unto harvest. Each of the boys was to represent a child from various mission fields. I was to play the role of a missionary and present the challenge of the mission field. What an opportunity to show off to Maria!

With my work and dating, I didn't have a chance to prepare adequately. I was to wear a pith helmet. I tucked my script into the bottom of it. The boys did a wonderful job; then came my part. I started off well, but about half way through I forgot my lines. I casually lifted my pith helmet and looked down. It was too dark to read the script. I hadn't considered that the stage would be dimly lit by a small floor lamp. I hesitated for a mo-

ment, walked casually to the light, and read the forgotten line. The rest of my part returned to me. While completing my lines, I put the helmet back on, strolled across the stage, arriving back center stage to deliver my final line. The laughter was so loud, I doubt that anyone heard what I said. At the end of the skit, I stood red-faced as folks laughingly congratulated the boys and me. I had turned a short drama into a comedy. The boys in my class thought it was hilarious and didn't let me live it down. So much for showing off for my girlfriend!

During our dating, Maria told me she accepted the Lord while visiting a church with her girlfriend. She knew of my love for Him, yet we rarely shared our faith. It was one more area where we failed to communicate prior to marriage.

Pre-marriage Forebodings

Looking back now, I believe even before our marriage, there were clear signs indicating that our marriage would not work. I failed to recognize them. I was raised in a poverty-level home. My father died, and I started working when I was twelve years old. I worked before and after school. She, on the other hand, was raised in a comfortable middle-income home.

Our family attended church regularly and was very active in it. My mother was a Baptist, and my father was an Episcopalian. They decided early in their marriage that we would be raised Baptist until we were old enough to make our own faith decisions. My dad often attended functions at our Baptist church. When dad died, my brother Al and I took over one of his jobs as sexton at Trinity Episcopal Church. We still regularly attended our own church. In my mid-teens, I began teaching a Sunday school class of younger children.

Until we met, Maria only occasionally attended church with friends. Prior to our marriage, we did not receive any counseling. At that time, neither of us clearly understood the scriptural teaching regarding marriage and divorce.

My home was a loving, caring environment with parents who were close and loving. After my father's death, my mother rarely left our home, but she always showed love toward us. Maria told me that her father was verbally and physically abusive.

My family liked her. Her father disliked me intensely and did not attend our wedding. He once said his family was casting a pearl before a swine. On the other hand, her mother was very kind and loving toward me.

I felt quite insecure in our relationship. Maria was more assertive and manipulative. On one occasion, when she became angry toward me, she threw her engagement ring into a grassy field. I looked for it for almost an hour. She stood near my car while I looked for it. When I walked back, she said she found it. (I was thankful she "found it" and didn't question how she found it.) I was very naïve.

After our wedding we lived the first couple of months in my family's home. We had our privacy. I learned years later that she complained a great deal to my mother and on occasion was verbally abusive toward her. I learned this from my sister after mother died. One of my brothers told me the same thing occurred when Mom and he visited us in Philadelphia. Until he told me years later, I had not known why they left for home early.

During the early days of our marriage, I felt happy and sexually satisfied. She was unhappy and complained, saying I was awkward and clumsy. I didn't know what her expectations were, and she never attempted to clearly define them. She was often upset with me and withheld sexual gratification when she felt that way.

When we moved to an apartment, she complained that it was not nice enough and was too far from her family and friends. This was in spite of the fact it was on the bus line, and we lived about as close to them as the distance I used to walk home when dating her. Most of our leisure time was spent with her family and on activities they enjoyed. I felt comfortable with her sisters and brother and enjoyed being around them. After we moved to our apartment we seldom spent time with my family.

Cancer, College, and Pastoral Calls

On our first anniversary, Maria had oral surgery and was diagnosed with terminal cancer. I was devastated and held my feelings from her for several days. I felt I could not live without her. She could not die this young. My life was totally centered on her health and happiness. Now my prayer life increased significantly. During prayer I heard a renewed call to the ministry. Shortly after that, a report came back showing no cancer remaining. We both interpreted this to mean that our Lord would supply our needs if we answered His call. We moved to Philadelphia, Pennsylvania, and I enrolled at Eastern Baptist College. I thought we both felt happy with the change.

The week I started college, our first son, Daniel, was born. As I was working full time and attending college, she ended up with almost full responsibility for his care. I believe this is when she began feeling bitter toward me.

Two years later I transferred to Providence Barrington Bible College in Rhode Island. We moved into a public housing project where several other student families lived. Living in this environment increased her bitterness and anger. I worked forty to forty- eight hours a week and carried a full college load. We had very little waking time together. I was neglecting her and my son but failed to recognize it. My focus was on my college work. This made her quite isolated, except for socializing with wives of other college students. We did go on occasional picnics and outings with friends.

Prior to the birth of our second son, Mike, we were able to move to a third floor attic apartment near a nice park. During my college years in Providence, Maria took my sons home to her mother's in New York every summer. I remained in Providence and worked two jobs. At the end of my fifth year of college, I lacked six credits to graduate with my Bachelor of Arts degree. That summer I added two classes at Providence College and made up the credits.

Six years after starting college, I graduated with two degrees. I received a Bachelor of Arts with a Bible major and Sociology minor. I also earned my fifth-year Bachelor of Theology in Pastoral Care and Theology. By the time I graduated, a pattern of isolation and bitterness had formed. This continued after I was licensed to preach and served in small churches. I had to work full-time to support my family. I was failing to recognize that supporting my family meant more than feeding them and keeping a roof over their heads. I provided very little emotional, social, or spiritual support for them.

My youngest son, Mike, had severe asthma. His doctor recommended that we move to a drier climate. I resigned from my pastorate and janitorial job at the State Infirmary. Our family moved to California. I became a social worker. A year later I accepted the call to become pastor of another small church. Once again it was necessary to work a full time job to provide for my family. I spent very little time with my family. I was back into the pattern again.

Here is a picture of how intense this was. During the first summer, I worked full time at the local post office; prepared for and conducted Sunday morning, evening, and Wednesday prayer meeting services each week; organized and participated one night per week in community visitation; provided home and hospital pastoral care; conducted memorial services; wrote reports; and developed an annual church program plan. In the fall I left the postal service and accepted a fifth grade teaching position at the local Christian school. Preceding and following school, I drove one of the "pusher" type school buses.

During this ministry I appeared before our denomination's ordination council and completed all of the other steps toward ordination, except the final "laying on of hands" service. At that point, due to the years of stress, my health began to deteriorate. High blood pressure, chest pains, and diabetes began to show their ugly faces.

With my health breaking and being unable to adequately provide for my family, I felt the door to pastoral ministry close. I returned to social work. My pastor friend, who was supporting my ordination, encouraged me to complete the final step.

As I would not be directly involved in full-time pastoral care, I decided not to finalize my ordination. I believe to have the title "reverend" before one's name is far too high an honor to be taken lightly.

My return to social work gave me more time to be at home and an opportunity to enjoy my family. During that time, things became a little more relaxed. However, tensions and arguments did arise over what my wife said was my lack of "strict" disciplining of the boys. I would try to talk with them and find out what had happened; why they did (or did not) do certain things; and see how we could help resolve the problem. Usually, in the midst of this, my wife would become very angry and say they needed a spanking. So here, too, we found that our views of discipline and child-rearing were in conflict. This led to many arguments and confrontations in front of the boys. Both of us felt we had to maintain our positions. I got the strong impresssion that much of her anger was because I hadn't helped with them in the early stages. Why was I butting in now? I should just do as she said.

As my workload increased at work and I became more active in our local church, I spent less and less time at home. When we were at church, things looked like they were going fine, but when we arrived home the stresses continued. This cycle went on in a downward spiral. The gap between us became wider.

Years of Individual Counseling

When my oldest son entered his teen years, he began rebelling and became a discipline problem. We sought counseling from a Christian psychologist. After two sessions, Maria decided that it was Daniel's and my problem. She would no longer attend the sessions. While tests taken at that time indicated she should be involved in the counseling sessions, our counselor decided not to make an issue of it. From that point on, she never participated with me in family or marriage counseling. Dan and I continued our counseling sessions. No resolution was reached, and Dan left our home. Of course, this did not bring resolution to our marital problems. I continued counseling with my psychologist.

One of the tests I took during that time was the Johnson Temperament Analysis Profile. The original version of the test covered traits such as areas of Nervous vs. Composed, Depressive vs. Lighthearted, Active vs. Quiet, Cordial vs. Cold, Sympathetic vs. Hardboiled, Subjective vs. Objective, Aggressive vs. Submissive, Critical vs. Appreciative and Self-mastery vs. Impulsive. My initial testing with this instrument indicated that in seven of the nine areas, I was within the excellent range, and the other two were acceptable. Part of our marriage problem was reflected in another test, which indicated my wife and I were near polar opposites in several major personality areas. After eighteen years of marriage, our relationship was clearly headed toward disaster. She was saying she didn't love me and wanted a divorce. My misconception at that time was that our marriage could survive. Our struggle went on. Christians should be able to work these problems out.

Over several troubled years, my belief prevailed that as a Christian, I should not be divorced. I told myself I still loved her. We could make it work. Even with my counseling, our two-faced relationship continued. At church we appeared to be a happily married couple. At home we were on a battlefield.

In an effort to save our sinking ship relationship, at Maria's request, I reluctantly submitted to amytal (truth serum) testing. Most of the questions asked were written by her. The amytal was administered to me. Then my psychologist asked me her written questions. Depending on the direction of my answers, he expanded upon them. Among other things, the findings supported my love for her, my feelings of failure in meeting her and my sons' needs, and guilt over the problems in our marriage. Clearly, I had come to believe I was totally responsible for our marital problems.

When I suggested Maria also have the same testing, she refused. She said she didn't need to be tested, as she was always clear about how she felt and believed she openly expressed her feelings. Her message was that "I," not "we" needed therapy

and counseling. From that point on, her focus in our relationship centered, not on my love for her, but on my failing to meet her and the boys' needs. This further increased my feelings of guilt.

We continued to argue over minor things. On occasion, Maria would become hysterical and throw things at me. During one such episode, she pulled off her wedding ring, threw it into the garbage disposal, and turned the disposer on. After turning it off, she took the badly defaced ring and threw it at me. This led to our first separation. It lasted a little over one month. My eighteen-year-old son, Mike, decided to come live with me. When she asked me to come back home, he opted to stay in the apartment and work at a local department store.

For years, my Christian beliefs on the sanctity of marriage and that divorce was not an option kept me in a marriage that should have never continued. I believe the damage done to my sons was far more devastating to them than a divorce would have been. Both sons had difficulties in their marriages. Mike divorced when his two sons, Bill and John, were in their pre-teens. Dan and his wife divorced after raising their two daughters. Margie, the oldest daughter, is an elementary school teacher, and Charlene, the youngest, is working toward a law degree.

Over the years we had agreed that Maria would work at home and care for the boys and the house. With both sons out on their own, she remained a housewife. She cooked, cleaned, washed, ironed, and did all those other things that can drive a woman in an unsatisfying relationship up the wall. My responsibility around the home was maintaining the outside yard and keeping everything working, such as fixing light switches, faucets, appliances, and our cars. Whatever broke down I either fixed or replaced. We never had a repairman in our home. Working a high stress job, I found it relaxing to putter around the house, even building additions, patios, and remodeling.

Our Move and More Counseling

At approximately the same time all of this was occurring in

my marriage, my Foster Home Services professional staff were evaluated and unjustly downgraded. They were social services workers III (the same level as child welfare workers III) being downgraded to social worker assistants. Against the wishes of my administration and the County Board of Supervisors, I was supporting their appeal. The appeal process went on for months. My workers won their appeal, but the Board of Supervisors called in a "hearing officer" who, in a matter of days, "overruled" the Civil Service Commission's decision. I was assured by our administration that the changes would take place by attrition. Instead, the workers' classifications were changed and their salary levels frozen. My perception of how to manage my six programs was 180 degrees different from that of my administration; thus my belief system of loyalty and respect for those I served would not permit me to remain. I began my search for a new job.

Shortly, after my return to our marriage, I was offered a new job in Santa Barbara. Maria went with me to Santa Barbara for the job interview. While she loved the area, she would not commit herself one way or the other to a move. When I received the offer she said the decision was up to me. After I accepted it, she became very upset and told me she would not go with me. After discussing it with my counselor and pastor, I decided to continue with my plan to move. She resisted, but then shortly before my scheduled move, she decided to move with me. This meant quickly disposing of some of our material goods and putting our house on the market. Due to the large difference in property values in the two areas, with the sale of our house, we decided to buy a nice used mobile home in Carpinteria.

Shortly after our move, I began counseling with Dr. Samuel McDill [2] , a Christian family and marriage counselor. In a Taylor-Johnson Temperament Analysis Profile done at that time, I had moved from quite lighthearted to very depressed, quieter, very inhibited, slightly more subjective, and less tolerant. It was clear that in a ten-year period, as my marriage deteriorated, so did my temperament.

I was thoroughly challenged and happy with my new em-

ployment and enjoyed the people with whom I worked, but my marriage was draining every ounce of my energy.

Our arguments increased, and berating became harsher. When she became angry, she screamed demeaning and emasculating remarks at me. After one particularly severe episode, I moved out. A couple of weeks later, she contacted me and asked me to move back in with her, saying that things would be different.

Deception, Disruption, and the Exit Door

A few days after I returned to her, she told me a neighbor had spoken to her about a couple who had decided not to move into their new mobile home in a park in Santa Barbara that had just been completed. Maybe we could approach them, buy it, and get a fresh start. I approached the couple, and they sold it to us. After several clearances and arranging a loan, we moved in. Things mellowed out for a while, but Maria began spending a lot of time with Mavis, a friend from the park. She spent less and less time with me. I learned much later that Mavis was the sister of the neighbor who told Maria about the new mobile home. In reality, Mavis had been the one who discussed it with her while we were separated. Apparently the reason she wanted me to come back was her desire to move into a new mobile home and be closer to her emotionally supporting friend.

In planning our move to our new mobile home, Maria said she would help me with putting the "skirt" around the bottom of it. She would pre-paint the wood for the carport and deck covers, which were to be built by a contractor we hired. After the move, she decided I could do all of that myself. With two handling the skirting, it would be a simple task to nail it in place. With one it was an almost impossible task to hold the long planks in place while securing them. After struggling with it, I designed a supporting brace for one end and completed the task by myself. For me to paint all the deck and carport lumber and stay ahead of the contractor meant painting from the time I arrived home until dark, and then rising early to paint before going to work. She spent her days strolling and shopping with Mavis. The rift between us became greater. The arguing subsided, only to be replaced with cold silence and occasional caustic, emasculating remarks.

We began sleeping in separate bedrooms. Our sexual relationship had long since ceased. Our situation deteriorated to the point where every time the smallest comment was made, it was interpreted negatively. An argument would ensue, followed by the silent treatment. Toward the end, I would come home from work only to be told, "If you want something to eat, you'll have to fix it yourself. I already ate down at Mavis's," or "Mavis and I are going out to eat and shop. You can get your own dinner."

During that time, another very embarrassing thing happened. Maria invited a couple of our friends over for snacks and fellowship. Shortly before they arrived, she said she needed to go to the store for some additional snacks. Our friends arrived, and she still had not returned. I got out some snack foods and tried to entertain the couple. George mentioned a game he would like to see, so we watched the end of a football game. After it was over, they decided to leave for home. I apologized for Maria not getting back in time to see them. Less than five minutes after they left, Maria came in with no snacks. She flippantly told me she decided it would be more fun to spend time with Mavis. That was the last time we had friends over to our house.

Mavis, her widowed friend, continued to be a disruptive force in our marriage. She helped make our situation get further out of control by bringing her paper down every night with apartments for rent, circled. I didn't accept their invitation to begin looking for apartments. Finally, one night I was met at the door and told, "I hate you, get out. I want a divorce!!" Our marriage was over. While my desire was to have the purified gold of a Christian marriage, I had grasped at straws, trying to keep a marriage together, and ended up with a handful of straw. In the raging emotional fire of a dead relationship, it was burned to ashes! Our house never became a home.

Some Reflections

As one who had several years of counseling without my spouse's participation, I am firmly convinced that to save a marriage, both spouses must be committed to marriage counseling. One spouse may begin counseling alone, but if the other spouse does not become seriously involved in the counseling process, the relationship is headed toward disaster. If the couple is Christian, it is best to seek out a Christian psychologist or marriage and family counselor. They are equipped both by training and Christian perspective to help sort out the pluses and minuses in a relationship.

While I did not stay in my relationship "for the kids," I should have recognized the damage our constant discord and arguments were having on our boys. If a relationship is not nurturing to children, each spouse must consider whether or not the children would thrive better in a single parent environment.

An article in the July-August, 2004, AARP Magazine, entitled "A House Divided," by Elizabeth Enright, speaks to the issues of divorce involving older couples. It indicates that a larger number of men than women remain in shaky marriages in order to spare their children. The primary reason given is that men believe they would lose contact with their children.[3] In such instances, where marriages are in turmoil, are the men more concerned with their own pain or that of their children?

Several years ago I was in a workshop conducted by a social work professor named Bea Sommers. One of her illustrations left a lasting impression upon me. She used a baby's crib mobile to illustrate the adjustment that each family member must make to keep the family in balance. Whenever a member leaves or returns to it, each member adjusts at his or her own pace. I can only imagine how badly children are thrown off balance when their parents argue, fight, separate, and reunite in cyclical patterns. Is such a living environment really what is best for the children? If this is the pattern, parents need to seriously consider divorce. Professional family and marriage counseling should be an intricate part of this decision making process. Whatever the decision, counseling should continue to support the family as they strive to bring their family "mobile" into balance.

Middle-aged and older couples considering divorce may find a study on the AARP Website, www.aarp.org helpful to them. It is entitled, The Divorce Experience - A Study of Divorce at Midlife and Beyond."[4] It is well worth reviewing.

A Psalm of Separation and Divorce

I was alone and in my distress I cried
unto thee—there is no hope,
Take me home, Lord, take me home.
My wife disavowed me—drove me out
then continued to rail at me
She and her friend laughed at me—At
the point of despondency
I cried out to thee, Lord—the room echoed
with my crying, my eyes were
sore, my heart sick—yet You did not answer me.
Oh, take me home, Lord, take me home.
My old friends pointed out my sins and cut me off,
I was an island of despair—despised,
rejected, isolated and depressed.
How can I escape? Take me home, Lord, take me home.
My soul withered within me, I cried
in the darkness of the night
I walked as a zombie through the day.
My work reflected the shattered,
broken thoughts of my mind. Scattered
papers covered my desk as though
blown about by the wind of torment in my soul.
My fruitfulness withered, the limbs of my
body hung down under the heavy
burden of guilt and despair—Are you
there, Lord, are you there?
The question throbs and echoes in my brain.

My wife says, "I am lonely, return, return."
My heart says, "Yes!"
My mind says, "Reflect!
What has changed? Have you? Has she?"
Oh, Lord, I need time to think through our
broken dreams and future hope.
Unless I or she—no—we can forgive and
forget there is no hope—our
marriage agonizes in the death throes.
Must it die? Lord, must it die?
I see her sitting there despondent,
despairing, her eyes are sunken,
blue eyes circled with red, rimmed, as it
were, with ashen colored eye lids.
She too mourns and suffers the pangs of
the death of our marriage. We
talk. Perhaps it can survive!
Her friend says, "She plans to wait, then divorce you."
My anger rises. Misled again.
I ask, "Is it true? Is it true?"
"She should not have told you that," she replies.
"But, is it true, is it true?"
"YES"
Anger, fear, rejection, loss, all flood in and overwhelm me. A
hurricane of torment whirls and swirls
about me. My soul cries out,
"Why, Lord, Why?"
The sullen, sunken, rotting corpse of our
marriage glares at me with hollow eyes.
My lips cry out, "If it is dead, bury it";
Oh, to pull those words back.
She speaks, "I will on Monday."
An apology does not help.
Can that which is dead be resurrected with a few words?
It is over, Lord, it is over.

Don Cunningham

Help Along Your Way – Questions for Reflection

1. What kinds of marriage related stress have you experienced?

2. As a Christian, what do you believe concerning the sanctity of marriage and the possibility of divorce?

3. Have you taken part in marriage counseling? If so, in what ways has it been helpful to you?

4. In what ways, either positively or negatively, have other individuals affected your marriage?

5. What factors must fall into place to confirm that it is time to move out and move on with your life?

Chapter II
Pointing Fingers and Helping Hands

It was the first Sunday following my final separation from Maria. I was walking across the church parking lot. A couple from the church asked me why Maria was not with me. I told them we were separated and getting divorced.

"Divorce, you're getting divorced?" he said, pointing and jabbing his finger a hair's breadth from my nose. "Christians just don't get divorced."

"Well, I'm a Christian, and I'm getting divorced, so I guess some of us do," I replied weakly in a state of guilt-ridden shock.

"I doubt that you are," he said.

He and his wife spun around and marched self-righteously across the parking lot to church. Stunned, hurt and angry, I stood there with, "Christians just don't get divorced!" ringing in my ears. Why was I so angry? His reaction was the way I may have reacted a few years before. Why can a person's pointing finger hit you as hard as though it were a cast stone?

My soul cried out, "God, do you still love Christians who get divorced?" In my broken heart, I must have known the answer. I continued through the sanctuary doors. The confirmation of this heart's knowledge was to be my quest as I journeyed through the valley of the shadow of divorce. I slowly walked into church and sunk down into a back pew. There would be no fellowship of believers for me for awhile.

Certainly, Christ told us that divorce came about because of the hardness of our hearts. On another occasion, he used the same term to describe His disciples.

> Later He appeared to the eleven as they sat
> at the table; and He rebuked their unbelief and
> hardness of heart, because they did not believe
> those who had seen Him after He was risen.[5]

Those of us who have walked through the valley of the shadow of divorce know the price we have paid, and are paying, for the hardness of our hearts. I believe it is possible for those who have not walked through this valley to display a similar hardness of their hearts in their judgmental attitudes toward us. Do they disbelieve God's promise that He forgives confessed sins and cleanses us from all unrighteousness, even the composite sins of divorce?

How sad that the people who have the most to offer to those going through divorce withhold it. There are some who even believe in doing so, they are honoring Christ!

Darlene Petri, in *The Hurt and Healing of Divorce*, reminds us that many Christians believe you cannot be divorced and still be a Christian. She also makes reference to many evangelists and Christian leaders who exclude divorced individuals from the ranks of Christianity. The divorced person is left in a no man's land between the church and secular society.[6]

Over the next few weeks, I found some of my dearest friends and neighbors choosing sides. Several totally rejected me. One of my two best buddies was told by his wife that he could have nothing further to do with me. I am certain he mourned the breaking of that tie as much as I did. It was one of the worst casualties of the death of my marriage. I'll talk more about my friendship with Glenn in another chapter.

While many of the church members distanced themselves from me, my pastor remained supportive. My friends at work were supportive and concerned. Sue, who always seemed distant when around me, noticed my depression. She asked me what was wrong. I tearfully told her I was in the midst of a divorce.

A glimmer of disbelief crossed her face, followed by a smile. "My God, Don, you're human!" she exclaimed.

In that moment, a whole new image formed for both of us. My tears turned to laughter. Maggie, my secretary, told me Sue frequently asked how I was doing.

I found other staff very understanding. It seemed like they found reasons to be kind to me. They seemed to sense when I was having a rough day and intervened in many subtle ways. I was invited to a lot of casual lunches, for walks around the block, and was involved in impromptu office chats. I was very blessed to work in a social service agency without the caustic criticism I was receiving from some of my former friends. My co-workers listened to me and interjected their thoughts. While sometimes they pointed out inconsistencies in my words and actions, it was done in a spirit of unconditional acceptance and loving humor.

My secretary, Maggie, and her husband, Ronald, were especially supportive. Both had experienced divorce and were sensitive to where I was in my walk through the divorce process. In a real sense, they invited me into their lives and home. Time spent with them was always uplifting.

Another Pointing Finger

Rita, a young Christian psychologist, and I had just completed a tedious, two-day facility audit and were returning home. It was a long drive back to Santa Barbara, so we decided to meet for dinner at a quaint family restaurant located about half the driving distance from home.

We were nearly through with our dinner when she raised a devastating question. "I cannot understand why you as an older, supposedly more mature Christian, whom I look to as an example, could be involved in a divorce. How can you be a party to such a sinful thing?"

My food formed a lump in my throat and then dropped like a lead brick into the pit of my stomach. "What did you say?" I asked, not believing my own ears.

"It hurts me, Don, that an older Christian who knows the

scriptural teaching concerning divorce can totally ignore it and be involved in a divorce. I'm offended by it," she responded.

As our eyes met, I could see that this young Christian was struggling to understand this apparent paradox in my faith and action. I was causing a babe in Christ to stumble! What could I say or do to help her understand? I wasn't in the midst of the agony of divorce with the intent of hurting fellow believers. I knew it would be meaningless to try to explain how for the majority of my thirty years of marriage, my former wife and I struggled to keep our marriage alive, but to no avail. How hollow it sounded as I tried to explain. Her facial expression looked even more hurt as she interrupted, "Those are just excuses, Don. You mean God isn't wise and powerful enough to heal a relationship?"

My heart broke as the words rang in my ears. There, in the midst of the large dining room filled with people, I broke down and began crying uncontrollably. I quickly excused myself and rushed to an empty lounge area. Rita followed right on my heels. She took my hand and said softly, "Don, I'm sorry; I didn't mean to hurt you. Until now I didn't know how deeply you were hurting over your divorce. I just don't understand, and I want to. How am I going to help other Christian divorcees if I don't know how you reconcile divorce with Christian beliefs?"

She and I talked until I gradually regained my composure. After my reassurance to her that I would be all right, she reluctantly let me drive home alone. As I pulled away from the curb, she pulled out behind me. Even though she lived on the other side of town, I saw her car headlights in my rear view mirror until I turned the last corner near home. She was a concerned friend who was hurting along with me. Her pointing finger turned into a supporting hand.

That weekend became another time of struggle and growth for me. The Lord wanted to teach me another one of His growth lessons. And what a lesson it was.

All night long I tossed and turned, struggling with Rita's comments. How could I keep a younger, weaker sister in Christ from stumbling over my divorce? What was my responsibility

to fellow Christians who had strong feelings against the sins of divorce? Over and over these thoughts ran through my mind. As I struggled with them, I became more and more depressed.

I am a person who is always up before dawn and can't stand to lie in bed. This day, though, I just laid there immobilized. Again and again I asked my Lord how I should respond to other questioning Christians.

Late that afternoon, a verse of Scripture, which we had discussed a couple of weeks before in our singles' Bible study group, came to mind: "Rejoice in the Lord always, and again I say rejoice."[7]

While I still did not have an answer, my heart knew the Lord had something very special He was going to teach me. While I continued to struggle with the question, I knew my Lord was preparing me for His answer. The depression disappeared, and an overwhelming feeling of joy came into my heart.

The following morning our pastor spoke on confessing our sins one to another. That afternoon, the text took on new meaning as I began to relate it to my struggle. I could see that I had dealt in a pride-filled manner with the initial pointing finger that first Sunday following my separation from my former wife. Over the months that followed the original encounter, I worked through the problem. My resolution was to graciously, I thought, forgive the accusing brother. How was he to know what I was going through? After all, he appeared to have a solid marriage relationship, so how could I expect him to understand?

My pride over being more gracious and understanding of my Christian brother's lack of knowledge had kept me from recognizing my responsibility to help fellow Christians understand how God deals with the Christian going through the valley of the shadow of divorce.

I had translated my cleansing and healing through God's grace as making me a stronger, more forgiving Christian than those who had not experienced divorce. I forgot that they were not guilty of my particular sins and would have difficulty understanding the divorce-related changes in my life.

As a divorced Christian, I learned through the experience

that I am not more complete than fellow Christians who have not been divorced. I learned that I have a responsibility to share the reality of God's unconditional love toward the divorced individual with them. Thank you, Lord, for those pointing fingers that became the supporting hands toward growth.

Divorcee Bound by an Oath

Another important facet of helping hands are the Christian divorced singles' support groups. Our group we called Single Persons In Christian Endeavors (SPICE). It became especially supportive to those trying to follow the command of our Lord in the book of Numbers:

> "Also any vow of a widow or divorced woman, by
> which she has bound herself, shall stand against her.
> If she vowed in her husband's house, or bound herself
> by an agreement with an oath, and her husband heard it,
> and made no response to her and did not overrule her,
> then all her vows shall stand, and every agreement
> by which she bound herself shall stand." [8]

One of the ladies, who had been a housewife for several years, found work and was paying off debts incurred by her and her husband during their marriage. She was struggling to meet the mortgage payments on her small home, utility bills, and food costs. Lois took great pride in learning new skills. I remember her excitement when she announced to the group that she had changed her first light bulb! With help, she gradually learned how to change light switches and replace faucet washers. Simple things, yet they helped her gain confidence in herself. As a young Christian, she was meeting commitments she made during her marriage and after her divorce. She had vowed to meet her obligations and become independent. It took a great deal of time, energy, frustration, and focus, but she succeeded!

Peggy had an even greater financial challenge. She worked for years, seven of which were spent supporting her irresponsi-

ble husband. He rarely worked and was always looking for get-rich-quick schemes. He handled, or should I say mishandled, their finances. Shortly before their separation, he convinced Peggy to withdraw all her retirement funds so that he could start his own business. In addition, in an attempt to keep the small business going, they took out a loan. The business failed. The problem was further compounded when he totaled her car. It was the final straw—she filed for divorce.

Overwhelmed with debt and receiving calls at work from creditors, she filed for bankruptcy. When she joined our group, she was bicycling to work. To make ends meet, some evenings and weekends she picked up soda cans along the beach. Every penny counted. The janitor where she worked saved the ends of toilet paper rolls for her. Even with this type of frugality, it took her more than a year to gain financial equilibrium.

About three years after her bankruptcy, she received a letter from the Internal Revenue Service. They billed her for back taxes, fines, and interest on her withdrawal of retirement funds. By then a close relative was aware of her plight and loaned her the money to pay IRS. She dutifully worked the monthly payments out in her stretched-to-the- limit budget. It took two years to pay the loan back in full.

She never received a cent from her former husband. Worse than that, he approached her, her relatives and friends for money to keep him going. By then they all had the sense not to give it to him. He left the area.

Our group was a mix of professional, white and blue-collar workers, a banker, office managers, and housewives. It made for a support group with many talents to share. When one of our members was overwhelmed by her obligations, someone in the group had either experienced a similar situation or had the professional skills to help her work through her responsibilities. Sometimes we involved support services from our community.

Members in the group had the sense to not just do something for the other person but to teach them how to do it. In helping each other, we tried to be sensitive to what amount of their own load the person could handle. In Galatians Paul told us:

> "Bear one another's burdens, and so fulfill the
> law of Christ. For if anyone thinks himself to be
> something, when he is nothing, he deceives
> himself. But let each one examine his own
> work, and then he will have rejoicing in
> himself alone, and not in another. For each
> one shall bear his own load." [9]

One of the greatest joys in our group interaction was to see members gradually work through their challenges and move toward greater independence. Some moved from being overwhelmed to finding joy in overcoming the new challenges they faced.

Sadly, this was not the case with all of our members. Over the years, some moved out of our area or found new church homes. The one loss that grieved us most was a beautiful young mother. We learned later that her therapist had recommended she become involved with a divorced singles' group. She came to a few meetings and seemed to enjoy the group. One evening, as she was leaving, she made a point of individually thanking each member of the group for the way each one had touched her life. Three days later, I read about her death. Her young son came home from grade school and found her hanging in their garage. At her memorial service, the pastor of her church spoke of her love for our Lord, her gracious spirit and Christian walk. He gave a beautiful, hope-filled message. The responsibilities she faced as a divorced young mother had been too overwhelming. How my heart grieved for such a loss as this. I took comfort in the Psalmist's words:

> "Truly my soul silently waits for God: from Him
> comes my salvation." "Our God is the God of
> salvation; and to God the Lord belong escapes
> from death." [10]

This loss made our group much more sensitive and protective of one another. With the heavy burdens divorced individuals bear, it is very important that we be very sensitive to their needs and state of mind. Using the resources within the group and referring to professionals with expertise in the specific area of individual need, in most instances, helps the person form and move toward meeting the new goals he has set.

Oftentimes a helping hand comes from those who have experienced the same kind of challenges. From experience, I would suggest in searching for a Christian divorced singles' group that an individual attempt to find one with beliefs compatible with his own. It is also important to know whether the group's focus is on supporting one another or on match-making. While over a period of time one may find a soul-mate in the group, the focus should be on the healing of one's heart.

Help Along Your Way – Questions for Reflection

1. How have friends affected your self-image?

2. How are you grieving the death of your relationship?

3. Who are the supportive people in your life, and in what ways are they helping you?

4. What can you share with others in similar situations?

5. What have you gleaned from Galatians 6:2-5 that affects your interaction with others?

Chapter III
The Walking "Corpse" of Divorce

I have heard that in ancient Rome, a punishment for killing another person was to strap his corpse to the murderer's back until it rotted off. Today, emotionally, many of us carry the corpse of a dead relationship along with us, much as the murderer did in Rome. We feel the weight and smell the stench. We toss and turn for sleepless nights, unable to rid ourselves of the burdensome corpse of divorce.

I see friends, divorced for ten, twelve, and fifteen years that are still carrying the decaying corpse of their former relationship. One of the ladies in our divorced singles group, after fifteen years, still believed that her husband would come back to her. He had left her and married her best friend. She felt that once he found out how deceitful she was, he would be back. She was unable and unwilling to let the corpse slide away. Time does not heal all wounds!

It has been much different for me. As I worked my way through the graveyard of divorce, I felt the corpse slowly drop away—bone by bone. That does not mean I didn't feel the weight, smell the stench, and toss and turn for sleepless nights. Nor does it mean that I am ever totally free of the memories. Over the years, little things occur that remind me of the corpse that was once on my back. However, when the corpse was gone, I was free from the past, able to live in the present and look to the future! I wrote the following poem when I came to the realization of what was occurring in my life:

Corpse on My Back

"What is that corpse on your back?" he asked;
"Covered with flowers, its stench well masked."

"There's nothing there, you're seeing things,
For naught of my past to me still clings."

"Yes, once there hung a body frail,
My very heart it did impale;
The bones have long since dropped away,
And now I face a brighter day."

"But, wait," he said, "A bone I see,
And it still lives to torment thee.
A voice from the graveyard of divorce,
Brings you anger and some remorse."

"Accept that voice as from the past,
And from your life it fully cast.
For then you'll find the peace it gives,
To know that corpse no longer lives!"

Don

What are some of the bones that make areas of divorce worse than the death of a spouse? Please note that I am referring to areas of divorce that are distinctly different from the death of a spouse. Through the grieving process, there are many areas along which they take a similar path. Having been a minister of pastoral care for several years and supported many in their grief upon the death of a loved one, I am not minimizing the issues of death. I also realize that there are areas in the death of a spouse that are worse than divorce.

When a loved one dies family and friends gather around you to help you through the initial steps of the grieving process. How different it is in the death of a relationship. In many di-

vorces, family and friends do not gather around you to support you through the initial trauma of divorce. Of course this will vary from divorce to divorce. In some instances, family and friends may have been involved in encouraging one or the other of the spouses to pursue a divorce. In my situation, I was three thousand miles away from my family. While they supported me, it was only when I phoned to let them know how I was doing. If it had been a death, some of them would have flown out to be by my side; not so with divorce.

Very few of the couples closest to us remained neutral and supported me throughout the divorce. They were also supportive toward my former wife. Never did I hear a negative word toward either of us from them.

As mentioned in an earlier chapter, this was not the case with some other old friends. The wife of another close friend, Glenn, used the opportunity to become verbally abusive toward me. She also used the opportunity to write to my wonderful mother-in-law to tell her what a horrible man I was and that my former wife was blessed to be rid of me. Her husband was no longer permitted to associate with me. This was very devastating, as he and I were like brothers. He was the first friend I made in the church after moving to California. Glenn and I met in a prayer meeting. The pastor mentioned his name as one needing prayer. I prayed for him, saying that I didn't know him but the Lord did. I asked Him to bring healing to his body and spirit. After the prayer meeting, he came up and introduced himself, saying that he was thankful that a stranger would pray for him. That night became the beginning of a twenty-year friendship.

During those years we helped one another on our projects around our houses, worked on building our new church building, were on church boards together, and even were teammates for over three years during our church's door to door visitation ministry. This is a man who was very shy but strongly loyal. Toward the end of the three years of visitation, I stopped by to pick him up a little early. His wife answered the door and told me he was in the bathroom throwing up. I told her if he was sick he better stay home. She responded, "Oh, he's not sick. He has been doing that every visitation night since you two started."

When he came to the car, I told him if visitation was making him sick he should stay home; there were other areas in our church ministry where he was blessing others. He told me, "No." He had committed to the Lord and me, and a little throwing up wasn't going to hold him back! To lose a friend like that tore my heart out, and I am certain it did the same to him. If it had been a death situation and not divorce, I feel certain we would still be close friends. I still mourn the loss.

Sometimes a bitter former spouse will do almost anything in an attempt get even for her hurts and to ruin the other spouse's reputation. Shortly before separating from her husband, one wife had cosmetic surgery to fix a deviated septum and shorten the tip of her nose. While she was recovering, she had photos taken of her black and blue face. So that neighbors would not know about her surgery, she remained in her home until the effects of the surgery healed. During her divorce, she showed these photos to family, old friends and neighbors, claiming that her husband had beaten her during their marriage. Such had not been the case. Many believed her. Apparently, they did not notice that the bump in her nose was gone and that the tip of it was less pointed. She severely hurt his reputation and caused him to lose several friends.

Another bone of divorce is the malicious tongue. It is, as James tells us,

"And the tongue is a fire, a world of iniquity:
the tongue is so set among our members, that
it defiles the whole body, and sets on fire the
course of nature; and it is set on fire of hell." [11]

A divorce seems to be the ideal spawning ground for gossip. I was amazed at how the rumors simmering around my divorce became like a raging forest fire. They ran rampant over my reputation, but were unable to conquer my spirit. It was also distressing to see the resultant change in attitudes of people in

our church and in the mobile home park where I lived. Unlike a forest fire, with the fire of the tongue there seemed to be very few firefighters. Many hearing the rumors became tinder to keep the fire burning and even pass it on! I learned that there is no more fertile forest for gossip than a senior mobile home park or a ladies' prayer group.

Several months after my divorce was final and my wife remarried, I met and began dating a young lady. A short time later, my supervisor attended a social gathering. A woman there from our church and mobile home park told him that the lady I was dating was the one who broke up my marriage. Obviously, this was far from the truth. He told me he knew I had just started dating her, but made no effort to correct the gossiping woman as he felt it might be out of place at a friend's party. Rather than help fight the fire, he opted to let it continue to burn.

I did however have one valiant firefighter living next door. She was a nearly ninety-year-old widow whose husband passed away during the early part of my divorce. Both of them had been very close to my former wife and me. We chatted with them almost daily, and I did little things around their house that he was no longer able to do. When my former wife remarried, I moved back into my mobile home and continued my friendship with her. Occasionally, she would tell me that another one of my neighbors had approached her with some new juicy morsel about me. She would listen to just enough to see what direction they were going and then give them her standard response: "That doesn't sound right to me. If you want to know the truth, why don't you ask Don about it? You know that's the Christian thing to do." I am sure she stifled quite of few of them, or at least showed them she was a fire retardant Christian.

One of the worst evils of the malicious tongue is that it is often concealed in the sweetest, concerned, most self-righteous faces. Sometimes it is revealed in the form of a prayer request. If one is really honest in his concern about a person, he will go to the person first and express his concern, learn the truth, and pray with him about the matter. This is obviously not the motive of the gossipmonger. Once again, James speaks of the tongue:

"If anyone among you thinks he is religious,
and does not bridle his tongue but deceives
his own heart, this one's religion is useless." [12]

He is basically telling us that gossip is of the devil and has no part in the true, Holy Spirit-filled Christian life. How many souls of divorced individuals have been demoralized and pushed away from the church by malicious tongues? Only eternity will tell.

In divorce, as in death, the financial obligations will vary from couple to couple. While we see many widows and divorcees living quite comfortably, there are many who are left destitute. A few years ago I sat with a widow during the cremation of her husband. In preparation I did a study on what the Bible teaches concerning care of the widow. In the Torah, history books, Psalms, Prophetic books, Gospels, Acts, and Letters, God makes it abundantly clear that those of the Jewish and Christian faith are to care for their widows. It begins with the family, the priesthood/pastor, and continues with the congregation.

Many churches preach very strongly on tithing. However, I can't remember a single sermon indicating what part of that tithe should be used to help the widow and poor (stranger within your gate). Tony Campolo, in his book, *The Kingdom of God Is A Party* [13] does an excellent job of relating Scripture dealing with the tithe and its use to help the widows, orphans and poor. I include divorced singles in that group.

Help Along Your Way – Questions for Reflection

1. What decaying parts of the corpse from the death of your marriage continue to burden you?

2. What are ways in which you can gradually let them drop by the wayside?

3. What similarities do you see between the death of a loved one and the death of a relationship?

4. How do they differ?

5. In what practical ways has your church helped you deal with the death of your relationship?

Chapter IV
A Weekend Visit to the Love Cave

Shortly after my wife and I separated, several of my old friends rejected me. Until then I thought we had a near-unconditional love fellowship. How wrong I was. When they did talk with me, it was with lectures on what a terrible person I was. They talked as if my divorce was the one sin they and God could not forgive. I was to the point where I was ready to believe it was true. Then I received a phone call from Ron. He told me his fence blew down and wondered if I could come for a weekend and help him repair it.

"Sure," I responded, "I'm free next weekend. I'll drive down to see you."

"Great, we'll see you then."

They knew my favorite form of relaxation was working with my hands and fixing things. The invitation was more for relaxation and fellowship with them than to help repair their fence.

Ron and Wilna were my dearest, most loyal friends. When my former wife and I separated, this dear couple was one of the few who were able to maintain a friendship with both of us. Theirs was truly an unconditional love. We met the first day we arrived in California. Though total strangers, we shared a mutual friend back East. They invited us into their home until I found work and a house to rent. For years we celebrated Thanksgiving at their home, and I frequently helped Ron with repairs around their house. They were a very intelligent, warm couple, but Ron was not very handy with tools.

I had a three-day weekend, so I drove the ninety miles to

their home on Thursday evening. Early the next morning I went out and assessed the damage. I bought new fence posts, some replacement slats, and other materials. By the time Ron arrived home from work, I had the fence post supports set in concrete. When the fence was originally built, the posts had just been set into the ground, where they rotted away. Saturday we bolted the posts in place, put up the cross bars, and attached the cedar slats. By evening the fence was up and the yard cleared of debris. We went out to dinner and relaxed the rest of the evening.

Ron was co-teaching a young singles' class at church, but his friend was to teach that week's class. Late in the evening, his co-teacher phoned, said he was sick, and asked Ron to teach the next day. He immediately began preparing his lesson. I headed for bed. The next morning he invited me to visit his class. What a blessing it turned out to be.

As we began the class, he asked us to get comfortable, close our eyes and relax. He then walked us back to some scene we enjoyed most as a child. We wandered through this beautiful childhood wonderland and then entered a quiet cave. My wandering took me past a little pond at Oakwood Cemetery through a small grove of trees and across a field of grass and flowers. Winding below me were the beautiful Hudson and Mohawk rivers. Slowly I approached my favorite place—Diamond Rock—where I found a cave I had never noticed before.

As I sat in the cave, I heard Ron say, "Your best friend has entered the cave and is offering whatever you want most in life. Take the gift and savor it in all its beauty." A few moments later, he said, "Now say good-bye to your friend and come out of the cave with your gift." At that point I found I could not say good-bye to my best friend, Jesus, for I heard Him say, "I love you. I will never leave nor forsake you!" What a gift it was!

When we opened our eyes, Ron asked if anyone wanted to share his experience with the group. It was amazing. Almost everyone in the group had asked his best friend for love. The friend turned out in most instances to be a parent or other family member. Many tears flowed that morning as each related how

much he desired an expression of love from that person. Most of them felt it was lacking in their childhood.

I shared my experience with the group. One young lady tearfully responded that she wished Jesus had been the one she invited into her cave instead of her father. She had never heard her father say he loved her and was afraid she never would. He was to have heart surgery that week. Ron gently asked her if she had ever told her father that she loved him. She responded that she had not, but she assured the group she did love him. As her father lived on the East Coast, Ron suggested she phone him and tell him she loved him. Later that afternoon, she phoned excitedly to say she called her dad, told him she loved him, and he told her he loved her, too.

What a wonderful weekend we spent in the love cave. The Lord was using my dearest friends to begin the healing process. They gave me a relaxed weekend. I did what I enjoyed and basked in their silent, soothing love. I had stayed with friends yet wandered the hills of my childhood. There were two love caves that weekend–their home and my cave at Diamond Rock.

Help Along Your Way – Questions for Reflection

1. In the midst of rejection, how have friends shown unconditional love toward you?

2. What blessing have you found in helping others while walking through your valley?

3. Write down some particularly disappointing aspects of your situation.

4. What would encourage you right now?

5. Bring areas needing encouragement into a quiet place, experience Christ's presence in your love cave, and receive His love gift. Accept His promise-- "I will never leave nor forsake you."

Chapter V

Lonely Apartment Dweller to Back Bedroom Grandpa

Cool it, Ladies!

My journey through the valley of the shadow of divorce started with searching for an apartment. I learned they were very hard to find in Santa Barbara. As I left my motel room, I picked up a paper. I always arrived at work before everyone else, so I began circling the few apartments I felt I could afford. Lord, which one do you have for me?

On my lunch hour, I phoned the ones I had circled. Only one had a vacancy. The manager said he would meet me at the apartment right after work.

I arrived shortly before he did. While I waited for him, a lady walked up to me and asked if the apartment had been rented yet. I told her I was waiting for the manager to show it to me. At that point he arrived. She ran up to him and said she was the first one there and wanted the apartment. Had I been edged out of the only apartment within my price range? The manager invited us both in to look at it. The lady continued to carry the conversation, not allowing either of us to interrupt her. As we walked into the kitchen, she noticed that there was no refrigerator. The manager told her the renter had to furnish it. She became very upset, told him he had to provide one, and went into a tirade. The landlord turned to me and said, "If you want it without a refrigerator, it is yours."

"I'll take it!"

The not so lady-like woman left, using a stream of language that would make a sailor blush. Thank you, Lord, for providing me with an apartment!

That evening I stopped by the mobile home. I picked up some more clothes, a lawn chair, a twin bed, a TV table, and a lamp. Once settled, I went through the used appliance section of the paper and found an ad listing a refrigerator for sale.

I walked to a pay telephone at a corner gas station and dialed the number given for inquiring about the refrigerator. A lady answered. When I asked about the refrigerator, she said she still had it. We made an appointment to look at it the following morning at 8:30 a.m. I returned to my apartment and circled a few garage sales. I would check them out after looking at the refrigerator.

I arrived at the upper-middle-class home and rang the doorbell. A woman in her mid-forties, dressed in a skimpy nightgown, opened the door.

"Good morning. I'm Don. I made an appointment for 8:30 to look at the refrigerator you advertised in the paper."

"Yes, I know. My husband is playing golf this morning. I have to take a shower. Would you like to come in and wait till I'm finished?"

"No, thank you. Take your time. I'll wait in my car."

While I waited for her, I measured the bed and header opening of my station wagon to see if it was large enough to carry the refrigerator. A gentle mist-like rain wrapped me in its warm, damp shroud.

In a few moments the garage door opened. She must have taken the fastest shower on record. She was wearing a robe and slippers.

"Oh, it's beginning to rain. Before you check out the refrigerator, would you like to come into the house, and I'll make you a cup of coffee?"

"No, thank you. I don't drink coffee."

"I also have tea or whatever you would like," she said with a coquettish edge.

"I better check out and measure the refrigerator before it starts raining harder," I responded.

The refrigerator was running smoothly and was cool inside. I opened the top freezer door and saw ice cubes in it. I measured the outside diameter and found it would just barely fit into the back of my wagon with a slight hang out over the bumper. She told me it was only about five years old and that she was selling it because they remodeled their kitchen. We bartered a little, and I bought it for seventy-five dollars. I tightened down its compressor bolts.

As I spread a blanket over my bumper, the robe-clad lady said, "If you want to wait until my husband comes home, he can help you load it."

"That's okay, I can load it myself. I've done it before."

"You can't do that yourself. My husband is a lot bigger than you, and he had two neighbors help him move it out into the garage."

I tilted the refrigerator on to one of its raised foot pads, walked it back and forth to my wagon, then tilted it onto the bumper. It slid very easily on its side into the bed of the wagon. It extended over the bumper. I pulled part of the blanket up to protect the finish and tied down the lid. It would keep it in place until I got home.

The lady stood there watching. Her robe opened slightly as she smiled. "Well, I'll be darned, you did it! Are you sure you won't come in for a cup of tea or something?"

"I have a lot to do at my apartment, but thanks for the offer."

As she pulled her robe together and tied the sash, I backed out of the driveway. I was entering the world of separated, divorcing singles. In less than forty-eight hours, two women had touched my life: one whose anger opened the door for me to get an apartment; the second, who made seductive passes, showing me that even when buying a used refrigerator, temptation could come my way.

My response: "Cool it, ladies."

Neighbors – Noisy But Nice

With the exception of short separations, it was the first time in my life I was living alone. At fifty, it would be quite an adjustment. Living in a one-bedroom apartment with thin walls turned into quite a new experience.

The first night in my apartment, I learned that I was surrounded on all three sides by noisy neighbors. Once I began interacting with them, I found out that they were also nice.

On one side were a mother and teenaged daughter who began arguing early in the evening. It was Friday night, and the young lady wanted to go out and have fun with her friends. The mother was adamant that she was mixing with the wrong crowd and would only be looking for trouble. The argument got louder and louder as they went in circles as if on a merry-go-round of controversy. Finally, I heard, "I don't care. You don't understand or care about me. I'm leaving."

With that, the door closed with a loud bang. I could hear the mother begin sobbing. Oh, if the walls were only thicker!

Shortly after that episode, the lovers upstairs began their love making interlude. As might be expected, their headboard began hitting the wall. I thought that only happened in the movies. Then came the crescendo of the climactic ecstasy. Young love was surviving. I sat in my quiet, near empty room and unwillingly shared in their moment of intimacy.

Finally, all was quiet. I showered and climbed wearily into bed. I dozed off, only to be awakened by the bang of the door I had heard earlier. The daughter was home. Apparently, she had been drinking with her friends. The argument continued then gradually subsided. A truce had been declared by the two weary warriors. I nodded off to sleep.

Shortly after midnight, I was jolted awake by a TV blaring in the apartment on the other side of me. I learned later that the man worked the swing shift and liked to relax when he got home by watching his TV until the wee hours of the morning. My prayer was that of a songwriter, "Let me make it through the night." So began my induction into the noisy but nice apartment group.

The next morning, upon my return home with my previously mentioned refrigerator, I reversed the process of removing it

from my car. I slid it up the three steps from the parking lot on an old, crushed cardboard box and my faithful blanket. Then I lifted it to its feet and walked it to my apartment. The manager came over and helped me move it through the door and walk it to the kitchen. I loosened the compressor bolts, plugged it in, and slid it into place. I turned it on, the compressor started, and it began purring like a kitten in its new home. My apartment was beginning to become home.

The misty rain stopped, and the sun shone as I spent the rest of the day wandering from garage sale to garage sale. I found a small color TV, some pots, pans, silverware, dishes, Tupperware, and a Betty Crocker cookbook. In our divorce, my wife got all the kitchenware, and I got my precious tools.

For the first time in my life, I would be cooking my own meals. Years before, when my wife was recuperating from surgery, I took my sons shopping for groceries. We arrived at the checkout stand with a shopping cart full of TV dinners. The clerk asked me why I was buying so many frozen dinners. I told her my wife had surgery and I was teaching my boys how to cook.

This time it would be different. I would make it into a fun experience. It became one of the most enjoyable things I would learn as I grew through my divorce. It was a challenge to try out several of the recipes in my well-used cook book. Betty Crocker, thanks for the help.

Each apartment had a small storage area in back that opened to the outside. It had no storage shelves. The apartment manager gave me permission to build shelves along three walls. I framed it in with two-by-fours, cut ½" plywood into 24"-wide boards, and screwed them into place on the framing. My activity drew the interest of my neighbors. While I was building the shelves, the young couple from upstairs stopped to talk. The wife thought it was great and asked if I would mind helping her husband build shelves in their storage area. I told them I would be glad to and gave them a list of what they would need to buy.

The mother and daughter introduced themselves. They

watched me work on the shelves for awhile and then headed off on a shopping trip. My nightshift neighbor slept through my project.

The rest of the second Saturday I spent moving all my tools and miscellaneous treasures from the shed at my mobile home to the storage area and onto the new shelves. Late in the afternoon, my nightshift neighbor came out and watched me unload my final wagon-load of tools. We talked briefly. He asked if my tools would be available if he ever needed to borrow them. I told him they would. He never did borrow any.

My Marriage's Death Gasp

A couple of months after our separation, I received a phone call from Maria asking if I could come over and see what was wrong with the clothes dryer. After work I stopped by to check it. It was working fine. I walked into the family room to tell her there was nothing wrong with it. She looked very pale and had dark circles under her eyes. It appeared as though she was suffering as much as I was! She told me she actually called me over to see if we could attempt to work things out. I would have to make a lot of changes. She talked about her loneliness, and I left feeling that maybe we should give it one more try.

As I drove out of the mobile home park, Mavis was walking toward Maria's. She smiled and waved her hand for me to stop. We began talking, and I told her Maria and I might try to reconcile. I was shocked when she said, "Don, Maria does not plan to get back together with you. She has the 'Petition for Divorce' already filled in."

I was speechless. I returned to the mobile home and confronted Maria.

Initially, she denied it. I told her Mavis said she had the papers filled out and ready to file. Who was telling the truth? She became very angry and told me if I didn't believe her, she would file for divorce the following week. I turned toward the counter where we usually kept our bills and correspondence.

There, lying partially covered by an envelope, was a filled in "Petition for Divorce." Our marriage was definitely over.

The following Tuesday there was a knock on my door. When I answered the knock, Mavis smiled and handed me a summons. Standing beside her was a smiling Maria. There were waves of emotion swirling within me. First there was anger. Then there was a feeling of betrayal, followed by numbness, on to depression, and next rejection. Wave after wave of emotion engulfed me. An overwhelming sense of worthlessness and failure pervaded my spirit for several days.

I decided that I would not respond to the summons by appearing to contest the divorce. I completed all the papers required of me by the court. Everything was divided equally. Maria continued to live in our mobile home. We had all of our documents reviewed by an attorney. Ours would be a so-called simple divorce.

Back Bedroom Grandpa

I lived in the apartment for about four months. My youngest son, Mike, and his young family came up for a weekend visit. During the visit they said they would like to move up to the Santa Barbara area. We discussed it and decided to rent a house large enough for the six of them and me. A new adventure on my journey through the valley of the shadow of divorce was to begin. I was to become a back bedroom grandpa.

I spoke with the apartment manager about moving. Due to the extra "fix-up" things I had done in the apartment and the high demand for rentals, he was willing to let me move before my lease was up. I found a four-bedroom home in Goleta and paid the first and last months' rent. By the end of the following week, we were all moved into our rental. I adjusted quickly to my back bedroom and the noise of a house filled with children. While it increased my financial stress, I enjoyed being with my son and his family. Mike soon found work, and the financial stress began to ease. His wife, Lilly, found work a couple of months later. Their shifts overlapped slightly, so I became responsible for the kids during that short period of time. When I worked late, my young, teenaged step-granddaughter, Lois, watched the younger boys. This led to a minor discord between us.

One evening, I came home and found Lois screaming at little Tom. I asked her what had happened, and she screamed at me that it was none of my business; she was in charge of the boys. I tried to explain that I was there to help. She blurted out that I wasn't her grandfather and retreated crying to her room. After giving her a little time to herself, I knocked on her door. Surprisingly, she asked me to come in. I told her I would like to be her grandfather, but that was up to her. Her folks would be home Saturday. We could all sit down then and work out a plan of what role each of us would have in the home.

Our first family conference went well. Lois was able to discuss the frustrations she felt in caring for her brothers while her parents and I were at work. She resented the fact that when I was home, I was "trying to take over," and no one had told her how she fitted in. It became a time of clarification of expectations. While I was to be in charge when Mike and Lilly were at work Lois and I would share responsibilities. We would use time-out when the boys misbehaved. Discipline beyond that point would be handled by their mom and dad. Lois appeared happy with the outcome. Being involved in the decision-making and having roles clarified eased her frustrations.

A couple of weeks later, while playing dodge ball in the back yard, Lois came over and gave me a hug. She smiled and said, "I really like a grandpa who is young enough to play ball with us."

As we adjusted to our family circle, I began taking walks with the toddler, Tom. One day as we were leaving for our walk, Lilly started laughing and said, "Tom is mimicking grandpa's walk."

Many nights I relaxed while rocking infant Joe to sleep. Over a couple of months, this became a near-nightly pattern.

I needed to be out of town for a couple nights on agency business. The evening I returned, I picked up Joe and began

rocking him. Mike came into the room, and I asked him if he would mind heating one of Joe's bottles for me. To my surprise he said, "Yes, I would mind." He then explained that the nights I was away, Joe cried endlessly every time they tried to put him in his crib. Over the next few nights I rocked him for a little while, gave him his bottle, and soothingly talked with him as I gently placed him into his crib. He adjusted rapidly to the new routine.

We lived together for almost a year. During that time we made many adjustments with each other, and strong bonding took place. I was also adjusting to the harsh realities of my divorce and my responsibilities in it. It was a time of life renewing growth for me.

Mike and Lilly found work in Ventura and moved there. About a month after they moved, my former wife remarried. I bought her interest in our mobile home and moved back into it. Once again I was living by myself. My adjustment and growth continued as I traveled the pathway through the valley of the shadow of divorce.

Help Aong Your Way – Questions for Reflection

1. What ways are you finding to cope with your changed living situation?

2. Have you faced temptations from the opposite sex? In what specific ways did you handle them?

3. What new things are you attempting to help with your healing? (Like Don's cooking.)

4. What approaches are you taking toward new s ights, sounds and experiences?

5. How are your family and friends helping or hindering your healing?

Chapter VI
The Shattered Platter

My thirty-year marriage was ending in divorce. I began to feel the heavy impact of it in every area of my life. It was as though my whole life collapsed in upon me. As the weeks went by, I fell into deep despair and despondency. Depression settled in like a dark cloud of morbidity. I was in the death throes of divorce.

I tried to focus on my work, but I found my mind dwelling in the dark recesses of despair. Even though my employer and fellow workers were supportive, I knew I was accomplishing far less at work than I should. When I arrived home, I would fall exhausted across my bed.

One night I was coming home from a meeting where I had been the target of two hostile factions. My last ounce of energy had been drained from me. As I drove through San Marcos Pass above Santa Barbara, California, I looked at the beautiful reflection of a full moon on the glistening surface of Lake Cachuma. What a contrast with the dark shroud of guilt and depression that encompassed my spirit. How could I go on?

I absentmindedly pushed a Doug Oldham tape into my cassette player: It was a song that spoke of failure in life, not accomplishing plans, being shattered, and taking the broken parts of our lives to the Lord, knowing that He understands.

While I had listened to the tape several times, I did not remember hearing Doug singing that chorus before. I pushed the rewind button and played it over and over again.

A river of emotions flooded my soul and gushed forth in tears. What release came as I found myself singing along with

Doug. The words of Jesus to the Pharisees, explaining why the Law of Moses permitted divorce, flashed through my mind. "…because of the hardness of your hearts." As I listened to the song over and over again, I remembered that the Lord is our potter and we are His clay. As long as the clay remains pliable, it can be molded. Once it has been hardened by the fire of sin in our lives, it must be broken. There on the mountain I saw the platter of my hardened heart drop to the floor of God's love and break into a multitude of assorted pieces.

How I had been struggling with the guilt of divorce. Christians just don't get divorced. Yet, why was it that even in the moments of deepest despair, I had sensed God's love toward me? Here, in my valley of despair, I had experienced God's mountain top of love and understanding. He was beginning to show me the path He would have me walk through my valley of divorce. It would be a path of picking up the shattered pieces, taking them to Him for cleansing, and using the glue of His healing love to put them back together. I began to feel an immense weight being lifted from me. For the first time in months, when I arrived home I fell asleep and slept straight through the night.

Divorce a Composite of Sins

Over a period of months, I read and heard what various authors and pastors said about their views on divorce. Some treated it as though the divorced person had committed the unpardonable sin. My more gracious pastor taught that it was part of God's kingdom age dispensation. Christians, being imperfect, could not be expected to live up to the standard. While this sounded encouraging, it didn't square with what my Lord was revealing to my heart; nor did it ease my feelings of guilt. I had not read in the Scripture where God said He would forgive a Christian for living in a different dispensation. He did say He would forgive and cleanse confessed sins. In I John 1:8–10 we read:

"If we say that we have no sin, we deceive

ourselves, and the truth is not in us. If we confess
our sins, He is faithful and just to forgive us
our sins and to cleanse us from all unrighteousness.
If we say that we have not sinned, we make Him a
liar, and His word is not in us." [14]

How that squared with what I was experiencing in my heart.
The more I thought on these verses and my broken platter, the
clearer the cause of my guilt and shame became. Within my
heart I learned divorce was not just a single sin, but a composite
of sins that contributed to my divorce! The broken pieces of my
shattered platter were not clean as though the platter had just
been removed from a dishwasher. No, they were from a dirty,
germ-ridden dish that had helped cause the death of a flounder-
ing relationship.

How was I to find the broken pieces, loaded with sin, and
take them to my Lord? My counseling with Dr. Samuel Mc-
Dill, a Christian marriage and family counselor, was going
well. In addition to his most helpful counseling, I decided to
contact the widow of the Christian psychologist from whom
I received counseling when attempting to save my marriage.
Fortunately, she was understanding and willingly sent me not
only my tests results, but also his notes. What a godsend! The
next few months, I prayed and poured over all the material she
sent me and discussed it with Dr. Sam. Through these insights,
I picked up my broken pieces and began to put my shattered
platter back together. Oh, the imperfections—no, dark sins—I
needed to deal with. How my soul agonized over those broken
pieces—selfishness, blocking, denial, internal anger, and inse-
curity. While there had been no marital infidelity, how far I fell
short of the admonitions in I Corinthians 13. What a large, dirty
platter it had been.

I scrutinized each of these sin areas in my life and forced
myself to see them for what they were. I looked at how ad-
versely they affected my marriage and confessed them to my
Lord and Savior. Cleansing and a new sense of peace entered
my life. The recognition of my sins in my life, which resulted in

the hardening of my heart and ultimately in my divorce, became a major healing point in my life.

Be Angry and Do Not Sin

One of the areas of sin that needed to be dealt with was anger management. For years I held anger in. It would raise its nasty head when my wife would nag and berate me. It led to heated arguments. The need for healing and cleansing became very evident one night during the divorce when Maria phoned me and began telling me what a horrible person I was. I told her she had no right to talk to me that way. She continued to harangue me, and my anger boiled to the surface. Instead of hanging up, I told her if she felt that way about me, we could sell the mobile home and she could find out what apartment living was like. Up until that time, I felt she was under enough stress and wanted to leave her in the secure setting of our mobile home. With her negative attitude and deprecating remarks toward me, maybe it was time to strike back—place her out of her secure nest. Perhaps in our divorce situation, I should begin behaving like the man she said I was.

I angrily hung up the phone and walked toward my bedroom. Halfway down the hall, the Lord spoke to me: "Don, be angry and do not sin." [15]

"But, Lord, she makes me angry," I retorted.

"It's all right to get angry, Don, but not to the point of sin," He responded.

For most of the night I tossed and turned, wrestling with my feelings and my sin. When I tried to rationalize what transpired, I found no peace or rest. Finally, I admitted that my attitude and response were wrong. I had become angry and sinned. Regardless of the provocation, my deliberate effort to verbally hurt Maria was sin.

The following morning I phoned her, apologized, and told her there would be no need to sell the mobile home until we both agreed that it was the right time to sell. Without responding to my apology, she attempted to continue her previous night's

Divorce is a sin composite,
My heart doth grieve and wants to quit.
In hardened arteries of my soul,
I let sins take their dreadful toll.

A hardened heart, shattered, broken,
The Potter's hand it has spoken.
Pick up each piece as it's my sin,
Let my Lord cleanse me from within.

Then I came to my Savior fair,
Confessed each sin and tarried there.
He cleansed me of my sins galore,
And told me, "Go, and sin no more."

My spirit leapt; I found his grace,
Each of my sins was cleansed— erased!
I could rejoice in heart and soul,
You see, His grace had made me whole.

Fresh tears flowed down, I found release,
My Savior brought me precious peace.
A special text, I now make mine,
'Tis First John one, the verse is nine.

Now free at last, my loss was gain,
As His blessed child I still remain.
Dear Lord don't ever let me slip,
And lose our precious fellowship.

This poem was written after my "Broken Platter" experience.

For those who would like to gain additional insights into this poem, please refer to Appendix A of this book. I have included Scripture verses that I applied to my life while writing this poem. The applicable verses are inserted between the ap-

tirade. I told her I only called to apologize, said goodbye, and hung up.

That experience reinforced the fact that it was alright to become angry as long as it was expressed in a constructive manner. Since that time, I have found that when I am comfortable with my own emotions and express them honestly to others, they usually respond to me in a positive manner. What an emotional release it is to recognize when anger begins to fester and to let go of it before it leads to sin. Here, in another important area of my life, the Lord's cleansing love gave me a fresh start in my interaction with others.

From Fear to Healing

The fear of being really known by others dropped away. New, more open and affirming interaction began with friends and coworkers. From years of experience and education, I had rarely hugged anyone. My cool reserve of not touching or being touched by others disappeared. I found myself supportively hugging others. Looking back, what a big step that was! Over the years, I have come to believe that hugs are one of mankind's basic needs.

During that time of healing, I came to realize that God was not only forgiving my sins, He was cleansing my life. As He was putting the shattered platter back together He was making it squeaky-clean. I was carefully checking each piece, washing it through the renewing of His Word, and piecing it back together with the bond of His love. My heart no longer cried, "Unclean, unclean." The inner turmoil was being relieved.

Nine months after my separation, Dr. Sam had me take another Taylor-Johnson Temperament Analysis Profile. There were dramatic changes from my previous tests. I had moved from nervous to more composed; from very depressed to light-hearted; from moderately quiet to socially active; from very inhibited to more expressive and responsive; from indifferent to highly sympathetic; from subjective to more objective; from submissive to mid-line dominant; from moderately hostile to very tolerant; and from very self-disciplined to a more moderate level. Six of the profiles were now in the excellent range; two were acceptable; and one was one point into the improvement desirable range. I was healing and growing through my divorce!

What a blessing and reminder He was etching upon my heart. In this clean platter, I would always see the thin hairline cracks and remember His great Love toward me in putting my life back together. Beyond that was my heart's knowledge that I had been cleansed of each one of those composite sins that had contributed to my divorce. I was free to grow. No, the growth had already begun!

On the one hand, I have heard some pastors and Christian leaders speak against counseling with psychologists and marriage counselors. In their opinion, it is a matter of getting right with the Lord. On the other hand, some psychologists and marriage counselors say Christians must stop using their belief system as an escape and face up to their emotional problems. They say these problems are not sins and thinking of them as such only increases our guilt. My experience is that much of what we term emotional problems are described scripturally as sin. Whether we view them as sins or psychological problems, to find healing one must look at them from both perspectives. It is only as we analyze how our behavior is affecting our relationships with others that we truly modify our behavior. I am thankful for well educated Christian psychologists and marriage and family counselors who help bring about healing from both a psychological and biblical perspective.

I have known several divorced singles who feel the guilt of their divorces ten and fifteen years after seeing divorce as a sin. Sadly, it is the sin of their former spouses that they focus on. They still blame them for their divorces. There has been little or no healing in their lives. As long as we blame our former spouses for our divorces and fail to look at our own contributions, we cannot know healing and cleansing. As we entrust our own healing to our Lord and face up to our responsibilities in our divorce, we open the door for our Lord to work in our lives.

It is crucial in this process that we have the help of professionally trained Christian counselors.

How about you? Do you view divorce as a sin or a composite of sins? Believe me, viewing divorce as a sin does not bring the peace of mind that we seek; nor does it present the opportunity for cleansing and growth, along with a fresh direction in our lives.

Where do you find yourself? Are you still in that dazed condition of looking down at the pieces of your shattered platter? Begin picking up those broken pieces. Take them to your Lord. For true restoration and happier future relationships, we need to search out each one of our composite sins and bring them to our Lord. He knows, understands, forgives, and cleanses us. I am thankful that Dr. Sam was there to guide me in that direction.

2 Poems
Divorce's Depression – Forgiveness's Delight

I wept all night, depressed alone,
For my sins He could not atone.
My heart broken, I wept and wept,
My soul by Him could not be kept.

I wept all night, depressed alone,
There were those who cast a first stone.
My heart cried out, "Where are you God,
Would I be best beneath the sod?"

Dreadful sin, in my deep remorse,
Could not keep it from its course.
Must I forever then remain,
Beneath its sinful, rotten stain?

Then one bright night a new song came,
It did my raging heartache tame.
It sang of broken hearts and plans,
And said to place them in Christ's hands.

propriate stanzas of the poem. As one experiences the emotional turmoil of divorce, it is important to relate to biblical truths as written by those who walked with God through the upheavals of life.

Married No More

Marriage over and nothing right,
I prayed to God in depth of night:
Soul in torment, torn askew—
"Guide me Lord, in what to do."

It hurts so much so deep inside
And I've so little of my pride.
I take my pain of sin to you,
And the sting of failure, too.

Though I've cried and screamed within,
You've told me I could begin again.
A message came as if out loud:
"My child, hide not behind your cloud.

Do not let your heart be stone
You were not made to be alone.
Trust in me to make things right,
Another lies lonely in the night.

Asking just the same as you—
How to cope and what to do.
You know I see the sparrow's fall—
So be assured, I hear your call.

Lie still, be patient, wait on me,
I'll direct what's meant to be."
A sense of peace then settled round,
When my trust in God at last I found.

Sharon

I inserted this poem to show how the very special lady, whom you will meet later in this book, used poetry to help her cope with the trauma of divorce. For her, like me, poetry helped her in the walk through the valley of the shadow of divorce. In both of our separate experiences, in our darkest, near hopeless moments, our Lord brought peace in the midst of our lonely journeys.

Help Along Your Way – Questions for Reflection

1. What measurable signs of healing are you beginning to see in your life?

2. What kind of support do you receive from fellow workers?

3. What insights into your life does the "shattered platter" experience give you?

4. In viewing divorce as a composite of sins, what are the individual sins, attitudes, actions, and emotions in your life that led to your divorce and need to be brought to the Lord for cleansing and restoration?

5. What role do you see a professional Christian counselor playing in helping you resolve these healing issues?

Chapter VII
Forgiving Those Who Trespass Against Us

Forgiveness is one of the most difficult areas to deal with in a divorce. Yet, it is essential if healing is to take place. The sins that couples commit against each other during their marriage and divorce are not easily forgiven. Some sins, such as berating, untruths and gossip, may even continue following the divorce. Over the years I have been asked if I have forgiven my ex-spouse. I believe that the term "ex-spouse" is a very negative way of looking at my former wife. To me, "X" denotes one who has been crossed out of your life, and the expression does not reflect a forgiving spirit. The question requires a much more complex response than a simple "yes" or "no."

I do not simply forgive myself or my former spouse for our divorce. From my perspective, as divorce is a composite or group of sins, so forgiveness must be sought and given to cover the multitude of specific sins we have committed. The seventy-times-seven rule applies.

When Peter asked Jesus how many times he should forgive his brother, He responded:

"I do not say to you up to seven times,
but up to seventy times seven." [16]

The question I raised with myself was, "What are the specific sins (negative behaviors and attitudes) I committed against my former spouse?" I had to seek forgiveness for these from my Lord, myself, and my former wife. For true forgiveness, there had to be a searching of the soul—a scrutiny of the heart to discern those hidden sins that lay within me. As they became clear to me during my review of my old psychological reports and in counseling with Dr. Sam, they were confessed, and forgiveness was sought. The Lord assures us that, as we confess our sins and turn from our sinful ways, He forgives us.

I found that the awareness of His forgiveness opened the door for forgiving myself. This came only after much agony of soul. Guilt loves to hang on, making it a struggle to let go. Release slowly came about as I took the broken pieces of my platter of life to my Lord. His grace finally gave me the peace of mind to forgive myself.

How often I prayed, "Forgive us our debts, as we forgive our debtors." [17] Had this prayer become just a ritual, or was it a prayer from my heart? If from the heart, it required action. True forgiveness, like love, must be acted upon. I approached Maria three times and asked her to forgive me. I sought her forgiveness twice during the time of our divorce and again following it. The two apologies made during the divorce are mentioned elsewhere. The one following the divorce was shortly before she remarried. She had not come to the point where she felt she could forgive me.

In my healing, I focused on my sins, attitudes, and behaviors that contributed to my divorce. Yet there were still those negative things previously mentioned that she had done to me that would fester up and cause pain. Gradually, as I grew through my divorce, I was able to deal with them, recognize them within the context of her life, and forgive her. This applied not only to our marriage and divorce, but to things done following our divorce. Whether a former spouse asks for forgiveness or not, for true healing, one must forgive as the causes of injury becomes evident to him or her.

Forgiveness needed to be given to others for the sins that contributed to the emotional and spiritual damage done during and following my divorce. This is an area no one ever raised a question about with me. Yet it is an important part of my healing and learning to forgive.

While some in the church cringe in horror over Christians divorcing, they fail to consider the damage they may be doing through their gossip, lies, and false accusations.

The Psalmist declares, "I hate and abhor lying, but I love your law." [18]

In the book of Proverbs we read, "A righteous man hates lying, ..." [19]

In Romans, Paul places "whisperers and backbiters" in the same category as those who have "debased minds." [20]

As referenced in a previous chapter, James states very clearly,

> "If anyone among you thinks he is religious,
> and does not bridle his tongue but deceives
> his own heart, this one's religion is useless." [21]

He portrays the tongue as an "unruly evil, full of deadly poison" and goes on:

> "With it we bless our God and Father, and
> with it we curse men, who have been made
> in the similitude of God. Out of the same
> mouth proceed blessing and cursing. My
> brethren, these things ought not to be so." [22]

As I recognized the damage done to my life by those who spread gossip and lies about me, it became essential to consider forgiving them. Those who would rather talk behind my back than confront me were especially in need of forgiveness. While I knew some of them, many of them remained anonymous backbiters. It would have been far easier for me to let God be their judge than to forgive them in my heart.

As part of His commission to His disciples, Jesus told them:

> "Receive the Holy Spirit. If you forgive the
> sins of any, they are forgiven them; if you
> retain the sins of any, they are retained." [23]

How crucial it was for me to exercise the spirit of forgiveness, not only for my own emotional and spiritual growth, but for their eternal good. Yes, "Have you forgiven your former spouse?" is a simple question, but it has a very complex answer. Those who deliberately gossip, tell lies, and backbite need to think of the eternal consequences of their actions. Oh, be careful, little tongue, what you say!

Help Along Your Way – Questions For Reflection

1. What people in your past relationships need to be forgiven?

2. Would you forgive them if they asked you? Why?

3. From whom do you need to seek forgiveness?

4. What are the actions and the attitudes from the past for which you need to seek forgiveness?

5. In what ways are you learning to walk in the Spirit of forgiveness?

Chapter VIII
Welcome to the Lord's Table

For several months I had not partaken of the Lord's Supper. The guilt I felt in the final months of my marriage and in the midst of my divorce prevented me from participating. I would be guilty of the body and blood of the Lord if I were to eat of it, as unworthy as I was. Rather than the feeling of fellowship and oneness with the body of Christ, I felt depressed and worthless. In the midst of our church's fellowship, I had an overwhelming sense of isolation. Several former mutual friends evaded me by quickly going in opposite directions. I felt like anathema was written across my brow. The church service, instead of lifting me up, was pulling me down.

In search of peace and fellowship, I visited several local churches, but none seemed able to reach out and meet these needs. So there I sat, back in my old church pew, depressed and watching the communion supper pass me by. Is this what God intended for divorced believers? Did His unconditional love run dry at the divorced person's door step? Were there no words of encouragement in His Word?

These thoughts of worthlessness and hopelessness went on for several months. Then came my wonderful discovery. God had spoken very, very clearly in Leviticus about where he stood on divorce in relationship to eating of His peace offering! There in the Book of His Law, He had expressed His unconditional love toward the divorced person.

In Leviticus 22, God Himself speaks of who may and may not eat at the priest's table. At least ten times in this chapter, God refers to "holy things" that are hallowed to Him. In Leviticus 22:13, the widow and divorced woman are placed on the same level of treatment by their priest father. The clear implication is that the divorced woman and her minor children should also be included in the circle of care. They are suffering from the death of a relationship. Fellowship around the Lord's Table is a strong symbol of acceptance and support, especially needed by those suffering along the pathway of divorce.

> "But if the priest's daughter is a widow or
> divorced, and has no child, and has returned
> to her father's house as in her youth, she may
> eat of her father's food, but no outsider shall
> eat it." [24]

The very meat offered to God and returned by Him to the priest shall be eaten by the divorced daughter! Imagine, a dinner planned by God, and commanded by Him to be eaten by a worthless-feeling, divorced person! Oh, what unconditional love flows out of the Book of the Law. How can the church, under grace, do any less than to invite the penitent divorced person to fellowship fully with it?

But to which of the sacrifices and offerings does this refer? We find the answer from the context of the chapter and in Leviticus 10:14 "…shall ye eat in a clean place, thou, and thy sons, and thy daughters with thee: … given out of the sacrifices of peace offerings of the children of Israel." It is clearly the peace offering. None of the references to the other offerings and sacrifices make specific statements about the daughters being able to eat of them.

The Expositor's Bible, [25] in comparing the peace offering with heathen sacrifices, clarifies that while heathen symbolism is similar to the symbols in Leviticus, it is man who presents feasts to God. In the Leviticus peace offering, it is God who provides the feast to man.

Let's take a closer look at the significance of this offering. Several aspects of its symbolism have special meaning for those of us who yearn to eat with the Lord and His people at

His table. Think about it again. God desired to share His bounty with us. He set the table, provided the meal, and commanded us to eat of it.

The peace offering was instituted by God as a sweet-savor offering to be presented for thanksgiving, at the completion of a vow, or as a voluntary offering. Is it not interesting that He gives a portion of that offering to the priest to share with his family?

As with all meat offerings, it was to be seasoned with salt. Barnes [26] makes reference to salt as showing God's eternal love toward His people and His unchanging nature. J. Vernon Mc-Gee [27] speaks of salt as a sign of faithfulness between God and the one offering it. He also sees the feast as always welcoming the returning Prodigal. So here, dear friend, we see the imperishable and incorruptible love relationship with God.

Another thing we note about the peace offering is that it had to be offered on top of the burnt offering, which was offered for atonement. Hence, our atonement forms the base for our peace and our fellowship with God.

In the peace offering, the person offering it was to kill the sacrifice at the door of the tabernacle of the congregation. The priest then sprinkled the blood upon the altar and burned the fat and innards on the altar. This was a sweet savor to the Lord. The offerer could take the breast and wave it as a wave offering to the Lord. The right shoulder was then given to the priest, who presented it as a heave offering. The movements involved showed that the unburned pieces were specially consecrated to God's service.

These two parts, after being offered before the Lord, became the priest's to be eaten by him and his family. The breast represented closeness to the heart, and the shoulder represented the strength of the Lord. What a special message to those feeling weak and alone.

The remainder of the meat was to be eaten by the offerer with his family and friends. The peace offering was a clear picture of God's fellowship with man and of man with man.

Man had the freedom to select an animal without blemish

from the flock of lambs or herd of goats of any age or sex. "Regardless of size and price," man had great latitude relative to the animal he was to sacrifice. This indicates that rich and poor alike could participate in the peace offering.

How God desires and is open to our praise and fellowship!

In addition to the meat offering, in the sacrifice of thanksgiving, the person was to offer unleavened cakes mingled with oil, wafers anointed with oil, and cakes mingled with oil. In addition to the cakes, he was to offer leavened bread with the sacrifice of thanksgiving of his peace offering.

> "If he offers it for a thanksgiving, then
> he shall offer, with the sacrifice of
> thanksgiving, unleavened cakes mixed with
> oil, unleavened wafers anointed with oil
> or cakes of blended flour mixed with oil.
> Besides the cakes, as his offering he
> shall offer leavened bread with the
> sacrifice of thanksgiving of his peace offering." [28]

In these two symbols we again see God bringing man together with Himself. The unleavened bread mingled with oil is symbolic of the sinless Christ, filled with the Holy Spirit. The leavened bread represents sinful man. Sacrifices were typical of Christ and had special significance. The peace offering has a prophetic connection with Isaiah 53:5, "The chastisement of our peace was upon him." It connects to Christ in such verses as Romans 5:1, Ephesians 2:14-16, and Colossians 1:30.

Lange links the Peace Offering in the Old Testament with the communion table in the New Testament. In I Corinthians 10:21, reference to the Lord 's Table identifies it with the peace offering in the old dispensation. It is a communion between the worshiper and our Lord. It is a feast of love toward God and man. [29]

Divorced Daughter Clean and Welcome

With all that said, now let's take another look at Leviticus 22:13: "But if the priest's daughter is a widow, or divorced, and has no child, and has returned unto her father's house, as in her youth, she may eat of her father's food; but no outsider shall eat it."

As I was unable to locate a commentary that spoke specifically to this verse, I raised the question of the meaning with a local rabbi. He explained that in Jewish law and practice, it was traditionally possible for a widowed or divorced daughter to return to her parents' home.

He further explained that the reference to "priest's daughter widowed or divorced, and has no child" was made not to exclude her but to show a distinction. If she had her own children, she formed her own family unit, and other portions of Scripture would apply. Having children and being divorced does not exclude one from the Lord 's Table.

Another statement we do not want to miss is the reference to "as in her youth." When the widowed or divorced daughter returned to her father's home, she did so under the same conditions of respect, obedience, and responsibility she had when she lived there as a child. So we, too, in coming to the Lord's Table, must come humbly and obediently, having examined ourselves.

> In Leviticus 7:19b and 20 the Lord says,
> "… and as for the clean flesh, all who are clean
> may eat of it. But the person who eats the flesh
> of the sacrifice of peace offerings that belongs
> to the Lord, while he is unclean that person shall
> be cut off from his people." [30]

> In Leviticus 22:3 He says,
> "Say to them, Whoever of all your descendants
> throughout your generations, who goes near the
> holy things, which the children of Israel dedicate

to the Lord, while he has uncleanness upon him,
that person shall be cut off from My presence:
I am the Lord." [31]

By permitting—no, commanding—the divorced daughter
to "eat of her father's meat," God is clearly viewing her as clean
and able to eat without being cut off from fellow believers (Leviticus 7:19 & 20) or from Him (Leviticus 22:3).

New Testament Peace Offering –
Examine and Partake

We should never regard lightly Paul's admonition to us in
I Corinthians 11:28-29:

"But let a man examine himself and so let him
eat of the bread and drink of the cup. For he
who eats and drinks, in an unworthy manner
 eats and drinks judgment to himself, not
discerning the Lord's body." [32]

Christ gave His body and blood as our sin offering. Upon
the ashes of His burnt sacrifice, we have offered our peace
offering and may have fellowship with Him and His family
around His table. As we carry the teaching in Leviticus over
into the New Testament, it is clear that we, who have examined
our hearts, confessed our composite sins of divorce, and by the
Lord's promise have been cleansed from all unrighteousness,
may freely have fellowship at His table.

"If we confess our sins, He is faithful and just
to forgive us our sins and to cleanse us from all
unrighteousness." [33]

 How we rejoice in His invitation to remember Him as often as we drink of His cup and eat of His bread.
I believe the Lord's intent for acceptance and healing by

the fellowship of believers has been clearly outlined in the text we have been reviewing. It is a message to the priesthood of believers that God accepts the penitent heart at His table. This illustrates in a very positive way how the church is to treat fellow believers growing through the trauma of divorce. We are to treat divorced persons with the same unconditional love that God and the priest's family displayed under the law in Leviticus. Can the Church under grace show any less love than Israel did under the law?

Certainly, Christ told us that divorce came about because of the hardness of our hearts. As we previously mentioned, He used the same term in Mark 16:14 to describe His disciples. Those of us who have walked through the valley of divorce know the price we have paid, and are paying, for the hardness of our hearts. I believe it is possible for those who have not walked through this valley to display a similar hardness of their hearts in their judgmental attitudes toward us. Do they disbelieve God's promise that He forgives confessed sin and cleanses us from all unrighteousness, even the sins of divorce? Man writes in chalk on the pathway of life. God writes in blood on the flesh of the heart. What man writes can be erased. What God writes stands forever. Dear divorced friend, welcome to the Lord's Table!

A Short Story - Mara

While reflecting on my growth experiences related in this chapter, I decided to write a short story to help visualize how the verses in Leviticus would play out in a divorced person's life in Old Testament times. I have included the story of "Mara" as Appendix B at the end of the book. When you read it, I hope it will help you grasp the truth of our Lord's invitation to have fellowship with Him and His family around the table He has prepared for you! (See Appendix B.)

Help Along Your Way – Questions for Reflection

1. What is the significance of the peace offering to the divorced person?

2. How does it relate to receiving communion in the New Testament?

3. What insights have you gained concerning the deeper meanings of communion?

4. In what ways does the story of Mara parallel your own experience within your church?

5. How has the Lord's acceptance of the divorced person helped in your interaction with your peers?

Chapter IX
Does Jesus Really Understand?

Many times I have heard and said, "No one understands like Jesus." Hebrews 4:15 clearly states,

> "For we do not have a High Priest who cannot
> sympathize with our weaknesses, but was in
> all points tempted as we are, yet without sin." [34]

But how could He know and understand what I was going through? He was never married, let alone divorced.

For many lonely, dark nights, my heart felt like it would break, and my soul cried out for peace. While I knew Jesus still loved me—something I never doubted—I felt He could not be touched by my feeling of infirmities. How I yearned to be understood. If He couldn't understand, who could? It appeared as though no one understood, not even Jesus.

Then, one day while I was reading in the book of Jeremiah, I came upon verse 3:8 which reads,

> "Then I saw that for all the causes for which
> backsliding Israel committed adultery, I had
> put her away, and given her a certificate of divorce." [35]

My Lord was divorced! He knew exactly how I felt. What a marvelous revelation that was! But I must know more. How did He handle His feelings regarding His divorce? What was His attitude concerning His former spouse? How does His divorce relate to mine? I was struggling with the feeling of rejection. Did God feel the same way when He was going through His divorce?

The first few verses of Jeremiah 2 recount the beauty of the relationship between God and Israel. She was His kind, young bride who showed intimate love toward Him, followed Him through the wilderness of life, and was the picture of holiness. In His love, He had brought her out of a desert of need into a plush, plentiful, fruit-filled land. Out of his bounty He provided for her. He took her from rags to riches! But all of that changed. In Jeremiah 2:13, we read,

> "For my people have committed two evils;
> they have forsaken Me, the fountain of living
> waters, and hewn themselves cisterns—broken
> cisterns that can hold no water." [36]

Surely, this gives a clear picture of one who feels the weight of total rejection from His bride—Israel. His spouse, whom He had nurtured, had forsaken Him. His bride, whom He had given the water of life, was trying to drink out of a self-made, broken cistern, rather than return back to Him.

Our Lord knew the heartbreak of rejection. His rejection by her brought Him to the point of trying to bargain with her to get her back. In Jeremiah 3:1 we read:

> "They say, if a man divorces his wife, and
> she goes from him, and becomes another
> man's, may he return to her again? Would
> not that land be greatly polluted? But you
> have played the harlot with many lovers; yet
> return again to Me," says the Lord," [37]

Here God is saying to Israel that she has done far worse than marrying another man. She has played the harlot, yet He wants to remarry her. God is so moved that He goes beyond the scope of His law to the depths of His love!

Does our Lord know the agonizing heartbreak the divorced

person is going through? Of course He does. He has been there Himself! In Jeremiah 3, we see that He has felt anger, rejection, confusion, and despair. The apple of His eye had turned rotten to the core.

You may be thinking, "Jeremiah is just using the symbolism of a marriage breakup with God to make the point of how far Israel has fallen." If this is the case, it becomes an even more dynamic truth. The famous theologian, Augustus H. Strong, refers to a symbol as being less, not greater, than that which it symbolizes. [38]

Whether we look at God's divorce as literal or symbolic, the wonder of the depth of His feeling and love comes roaring through. He is touched by the feeling of our infirmities, even in the death of a relationship. To be thrilled at what lies in store for us, we only need to contemplate the beauty of becoming the bride of Christ. We have a relationship with Him that is eternal. He loves us with an everlasting love! Oh, yes, Jesus understands!

Divorce and God's Grace

For months I struggle—really grope,
A divorced person without hope.
My world exploded—blown apart,
My sins have broken my hard heart.

Friends departed, I am alone,
Even God's grace cannot atone.
Divorce has come through my cold heart.
My sins keep God and me apart.

If divorce is beyond God's grace,
I must run a grief-stricken race.
My heart and soul are in despair,
Can it be that God does not care?

Don E. Cunningham

He says He heals the broken heart,
And gives us all a fresh new start.
And yet I hear preachers proclaim,
"You, the divorced, must bear your shame!"

Mind and soul confused, in distress,
Who will save me from my mess?
God forgives murderer and thief,
Yet His grace cannot spare my grief.

Can it be that my God is dead?
In His word this I never read.
His Spirit's Love touches my heart,
"I still love you; we'll never part."

Death of marriage His voice still heard,
"Child, please study my precious Word.
In Scripture my truth is revealed,
Study its pages and be healed."

I studied its pages and found
Sin abounded, grace more abounds.
Does it work with sins of divorce?
Can it be He shares my remorse?

I look in His law, find His grace,
Great tears of joy flow down my face.
Divorced daughter at table eats,
Sits with priest father, shares his meats!

Christ never divorced. Can it be,
He was tempted and tried like me?
Look to the prophets in remorse,
Their words show God got a divorce!

Christ gives body for me and you,
Sins forgiven through His blood, too.
Man of sorrows, stricken with grief,
Brings me forgiveness—sweet relief!

Yes, a hardened heart has been healed,
As it was broken, sins revealed.
Christ helped me see them—I confessed,
Then He forgave me, cleansed and blessed.

Don

For those who would like to meditate on this poem using verses of Scripture I reflected upon while writing each stanza, please refer to Appendix C. In it are applicable verses placed between each stanza. The Scripture helps one understand that God's Word is with us each step of the way as we walk through the valley of the shadow of divorce.

Help Along Your Way – Questions for Reflection

1. How does Scripture demonstrate that our Lord understands the heartbreak of the divorced Christian? (See Hebrews 4:15, Jeremiah 2 and 3.)

2. What feelings do you have that are similar to those expressed by our Lord in Jeremiah 2 and 3?

3. With which verses of Scripture reflected upon in relationship to the poem, "Divorce and God's Grace" do you best identify?

4. How do these verses help you in your daily walk?

5. Can you share your deepest despair and disappointments with the Lord today?

Chapter X
Bound by a Band

It had twisted and turned on the right ring finger of my left hand for over thirty years. Over the years, everything from broom handles to dead bodies had worn away the specially engraved design on its outer surface. I had worked as a janitor from age twelve through college. For a time I moonlighted for a local undertaker. As the ring had never been taken off during all the years of my marriage, I thought the engraving on the inside was about as clear as the day I put it on—LOVE-DEC-MKV - 11/6/49.

As the luster had worn off the outside of the ring, so had it also deteriorated off my marriage. Now facing the impending finalization of my divorce, I was focusing on the ring of love on my finger. It was a perfect circle, the symbol of love without end.

One day while on break with a friend at work, he asked, "How come you're still wearing your wedding band? After all, your marriage is over."

"My divorce isn't final until the end of December; I'll wear it 'til then," I snapped.

A few days later, at a divorced singles planning meeting, a member of the group queried, "Don, how can you be a leader of our group when you don't identify yourself as a member of it?'

"I certainly do!" I responded, somewhat irritated.

"No, you don't. You still act like you are married."

"How do you figure that?" I was becoming very agitated.

"You're still wearing your wedding band."

"What difference does that make? It's only a symbol; I'll take it off when my divorce is final in December."

About a week later, after a restless, sleepless night, I sat at my desk and tried to concentrate, but to no avail. As I sat there, trying to think, I subconsciously reached down to twist my wedding ring. It was a nervous habit I had developed over the years. Oh, NO! The ring was gone! The ring I had never taken off my finger had disappeared.

I looked through the papers on my desk, looked around on the floor, and frantically searched through all my pockets. I pulled all the change and keys out and put them on my desk. The ring wasn't mixed in with them. I began to feel a sticky, cold sweat envelop me. Where could the ring be? I retraced my steps back to my car. I looked around and in it. No ring. Where could it be? How could I have lost it after all these years?

Irrational thoughts struck me. "If only I hadn't lost all that weight, my finger would still be too fat for it to have fallen off."

Maybe it came off when I shaved this morning. If only I hadn't begun to use that greasy brushless shaving cream, my finger wouldn't have been so slippery.

Oh, no; maybe it went down into the sink drain?

"What will I do?" I thought. "The phone company hasn't installed a phone at the house yet, so I can't phone my daughter-in-law to look for it."

Just then Maggie, my secretary, walked in. "What's the matter, Don? You look sort of sick."

"I lost my wedding ring."

"So, it's only a symbol of marriage, and yours is over."

How different that sounded when she said it.

"But I wore it for thirty years. It's never been off my finger, and my divorce isn't final yet."

My voice became a little higher pitched and strained. Maggie, as sensitive and supportive as she was, immediately picked up on how stressed out I was. "Ron has already left for work, but why don't you call Joan? I'm sure she wouldn't mind dashing over to your house."

She was a fellow worker who was off work on maternity leave. I quickly dialed her number. It seemed as though she would never answer, but finally her sleepy voice said, "Good morning."

I told her my dilemma. She couldn't go over for me, as her infant was ill. She said she would call another friend of hers for me and ask her to stop by my house on her way to work. My daughter-in-law, Lilly, could look for it and call me from a pay phone.

I became so preoccupied with where I could have lost my ring that I couldn't concentrate on my work. What was taking her so long to call me? Finally, after about an hour, she called. She had double-checked my bedroom, bathroom, and overstuffed chair, but she could not find it. Hearing the stress in my voice, Lilly said she would go right home and continue looking for it.

Throughout the day, I found myself unable to focus on my work. Where could I have lost my ring? I spent my lunch hour searching and re-searching through my car. It was nowhere to be found. My missing ring held me in its circled, unending grasp all day long. Did I possess it, or did it possess me?

After work I hurried home and wearily searched every place I could think of. I checked the bed, bedding, in the folds of my chair, the carpeting, and the kitchen area—all to no avail. Finally, I took apart the sink trap hoping that I might find it there. I found nothing but hair and slime. Each new area searched made me feel more and more depressed. I fell across my bed and cried. My wedding ring was gone.

I lay there sobbing and thought about my lost ring and the comments made about me still wearing it. "It's only a symbol," but it had me in its clutches. I was held by it in such a way that I could not let it go. It was the last vestige of a marriage I had hoped would be the ongoing fulfillment of love.

I wrestled back and forth between "the ring is gone" and "the marriage is over." It's gone, it's over, but it isn't even December yet. It is gone, it is over!

It had been a stressful, fatiguing day. Exhausted, I got up, took a shower, and headed for bed early. I slid beneath the covers and rolled over on my side. As I did, I felt a small object against my hip. Quickly, I turned on the light and rolled the blanket down. As I smoothed out the sheets, there in a folded over crease was my lost ring!

I picked it up and looked at—"LOVE, DEC-MKV-11/6/49." The inscription was much more worn than I had thought. Just as the design on my ring had disappeared, so too had the love in my marriage faded. Slowly, I dropped the ring into my jewelry box. I was no longer bound by a band. After all, it was ONLY A SYMBOL!

What should I do with this band that held me captive for so many years?

Help Along Your Way – Questions for Reflection

1. What are the symbols and experiences from your past that keep you from moving forward?

2. How can you take them and use them as symbols of your new life?

3. What challenges give you anxiety about your new life?

4. What is the next step of faith the Lord is asking you to take?

5. Have you committed the outcome of your life into our Lord's hands?

Chapter XI
To Remain Single or Remarry – That Is the Question

Even though Maria had remarried and there was no possibility of us getting back together, I had not been dating. I was to the point in my healing process where I was ready to move from the past to the future. I had passed through the valley of the shadow of divorce and was moving toward the hope of what lay before me.

Questions began to swirl in my mind. What is God's will for my life? Is it that I remain single? Should I consider remarriage? If I were to remarry, what would I look for in a wife? As I enjoy poetry, I began to write a poem about what I would look for in a wife. I wrote a couple of lines when the Lord spoke to my heart.

"Wait a minute, Don. You're getting ahead of yourself. The question is not what you want in a wife, but what do you have to offer a wife?"

I am so prone to get things backward, to put me first. Before thinking about what I would look for in a wife, it was essential for me to take a realistic look at myself. Why should I assume God's plan for my life, at that point, was to remarry? How easily I was forgetting that it was the Lord who was cleansing and putting my platter back together.

As I looked again at the restored platter of my life, I could see those areas that I had identified, confessed, and received healing. If I really believed in God's forgiveness and healing, then the areas of my personality that were contributors to my divorce were now areas that I could view as strengths. Strengths, that is, in the sense that they were cleansed areas upon which I could build more wholesome relationships, be they as a single or married person.

One such area was in the display of emotions. For years I had been a very internal person who rarely expressed how I felt. Over a long period of time, I learned it was futile to express my feelings. It only led to more hurt and rejection.

Contrary to my experience, the Scriptures often speak of our emotions. We are told to "Rejoice with those who rejoice, and weep with those who weep." [39] The shortest verse in the Scriptures gives us a powerful demonstration of God's emotions when it simply says, "Jesus wept." [40]

Over the months, as God's love and forgiveness shined upon me, I recognized that my emotions were valid. They were to be positively expressed, not kept inside. I was to share them in my interaction with others.

In my daily communication with others, I began to use more feeling words. With the verbal openness, I felt more accepted and understood. I had many hugs when growing up. These disappeared during my marriage. Hugging returned as an important part of my life. I found when I hugged someone it brought a feeling of openness, warmth, and acceptance between us. It was the cry of one soul to another saying, "Hey, I know how you feel. I'm here to support you." What a wonderful growing experience it was for me when I learned to be open and unafraid of sharing my life with others!

Other areas that had been healed were feelings of anger and bitterness. I had been able to unconditionally forgive myself, Maria, Mavis, and others who had played negative roles during and after my divorce. I had heard Paul's admonition to the Ephesians and applied it to my life:

"Let all bitterness, wrath, anger, clamor,
and evil speaking be put away from you,
with all malice. And be kind to one another,
tenderhearted, forgiving one another, even
as God in Christ forgave you." [41]

My Lord in His love had tenderized my once-hardened heart. I was interacting with others in the manner our Lord had intended me to do. I was ready to move on.

For months I struggled with what the Scriptures taught regarding divorce and remarriage. What was God's plan for me? In Matthew, Jesus spoke very pointedly with the Pharisees concerning divorce and remarriage. He clearly was opposed to both. [42] However, when His disciples said to Him,

"If such is the case of the man with his wife, it is better not to marry."

Jesus responded to them, "All cannot accept this saying, but only those to whom it has been given: For there are eunuchs who were born thus from their mother's womb, and there are eunuchs who were made eunuchs by men, and there are eunuchs who have made themselves eunuchs for the kingdom of heaven's sake. He who is able to accept it, let him accept it." [43]

I know there are many who hold to the position that the question raised was only in relationship to marriage. However, it seems to me, as the disciples raised the issue following a discussion of divorce and remarriage, Christ's response could be seen within the full context of marriage, divorce, and remarriage. If this were the case, then some men were intended to be married and others to remain single. Could I accept being single?

The final question became, "Could I best serve Him as a single or married man?" I remember very clearly on a Thursday evening, while in prayer, a statement by God in Genesis imprinted itself upon my mind.

"And the Lord God said, "It is not good that man should be alone; I will make him a helper comparable to him." [44]

This, along with having looked at my strengths and weaknesses both as a single man and what I would have to offer as a married man, I received peace that I could serve my Lord better in the married state. I became comfortable with the idea of dating and the possibility of remarriage. Would He give me a helper compatible with myself?

Don E. Cunningham

So Let Me Love

As I pondered about my life,
Asked, "What do I want in a wife?"
Then the thought broke in from the blue,
"What would a wife look for in you?"

A longing to communicate,
A life filled with love, never hate.
Minister to her precious soul,
And make our relationship whole.

Be sensitive to her every mood,
Tender questions never allude.
To see her as my spotless bride,
To hold her near—stand by her side.

To cherish every special dream,
And live together as a team.
To love—caress so tenderly,
Lift up her heart in ecstasy.

To wipe away her glistening tears,
And protect her from hidden fears.
To rub her back and hold her hand,
And let her know I understand.

Now as I look deep down inside,
Holy Spirit, please be my guide.
To be the man I need to be,
I'll need your caring love, You see.

May I so live my fleeting life,
Solely to love my chosen wife,
That when my soul flies up above,
My wife can say, "Oh, how he loved!"

Don

Help Along Your Way – Questions for Reflection

1. What are the issues you feel must be resolved to move toward a new relationship?

2. What are the factors you must consider to determine whether to remain single or remarry?

3. What role do God, prayer, and Scripture play in this decision?

4. What scriptural guidelines will help you in this decision?

5. What role do personal abilities and desires play in making your decision?

Chapter XII
Behold My Special Princess

She sat silently, alone, at the end of the long empty row of chairs. This beautiful blonde with tresses of hair flowing gently down to the tips of her shoulders instantly caught my eye. When I entered the room, she turned and smiled a pleasant smile, accented by her pearly white teeth and blue-grey eyes. We introduced ourselves and began chatting. Her name was Sharon, the flower of the plain, a vision of beauty. She had been attending the class for six months, but this was the first Sunday I noticed her. How could I have missed seeing her until now? It seemed odd that I should notice her the Sunday following my Thursday prayer experience.

As we talked, Sharon mentioned that she was in the process of divorce. In fact, her divorce would be final the following Friday. I invited her to attend our church sponsored divorced singles group, Single Persons in Christian Endeavors (SPICE), which met in my mobile home. I also mentioned that the day the Judgment of Final Dissolution of Marriage arrived was very traumatic for me. It was not good to be alone. I offered to take her out to dinner. She softly responded that she would think about it, but she didn't feel the finalization of her divorce would be that traumatic.

By that time the room was filling up, and the Bible teacher finished writing his outline on the board. The class session was ready to begin. My mind, of course, was on the beautiful blonde sitting across the aisle from me. Sharon seemed to be a very sweet, soft-spoken young lady.

The following Tuesday, our SPICE group met. We started a

little late, and Sharon still had not arrived. I began to wonder if she would come to the meeting. Then there was a soft rap on the back door. I opened the door, and there she stood in her nurse's uniform. She had to work late, so she rode her bike directly to the meeting.

During the social time following our Bible study, I once again told her it would not be good for her to be alone Friday evening, and I would be glad to take her to dinner. Once again she responded that she was certain she was going to be fine, but if I was asking her for a date, she would be happy to go out to dinner with me. Boy, how awkward I was at re-entering the dating world. How sensitive she was to what I was trying to say! Some time later she told me at first she thought I was offering her a "charity" date, but she realized I was trying to be helpful.

The rest of the week seemed to drag. I was like a teenager going on his first date. Of course, when my secretary heard I was going out on a date, the warm-hearted teasing began. One day I mentioned to her I wasn't even certain what to wear. I was probably the worst dressed person in the office. My clothes were never coordinated. She outlined for me what would match and look good on me. Thank the Lord for my empathetic secretary with a creative flair!

Finally, Friday arrived. I had to go out of town to a meeting. Wouldn't you know, my return flight landed late. She didn't have a phone, so I couldn't tell her I would be late. When we finally touched down, I rushed home, showered, shaved, and dressed quickly.

A Quiet Dinner

When I arrived at her modest apartment, she was patiently waiting and ready to go. How beautiful she looked. We drove to the Miramar Restaurant in Montecito. As we drove there, we talked mostly about our Sunday school class and our work. At the restaurant, the maitre-d' seated us near a window overlooking a garden and swimming pool. A full moon reflected from the pool's surface. On the table, a little candle in a red goblet

glimmered. As it flickered, it sent dancing rays of light across her face. One moment it highlighted her radiant smile, then flashed upon her golden hair, then leapt back to her lips and lovely white teeth. It, like me, could not absorb her beauty and grace. How blessed I was to be sitting there with her!

As we sat talking, a thousand thoughts raced back and forth across my mind. How young she looks. Is she too young to be going out with me? Is she enjoying herself? Does she feel comfortable with me? What should we talk about? Do I look alright? Do my clothes really match? What does she think about me? What kind of things does she enjoy doing? It was really awkward being a middle-aged teenager on my first date in over thirty years.

While the meal progressed, we gradually became more comfortable with each other. We found that we both enjoyed similar activities: reading, poetry, music, working with our hands, and walking.

During our drive back to her apartment, we talked more about ourselves, revealing a little bit about our past experiences and hopes for the future. When we arrived at her apartment, I invited her to go with me and our SPICE group to a picnic at the beach the following day. She accepted! I thanked her for a pleasant evening and then waited for her to go inside and to hear her lock the door. When I arrived home, I couldn't get my mind off this wonderful lady. For the first time in years, I sat down and wrote a poem expressing my strong, warm feelings. How good it felt! A couple of days later when I shared my poem with her, she broke into laughter and handed me the one she had written. Interestingly, she addressed the same areas I had, only from a woman's perspective. Apparently, not only do great minds run in the same channel, so do minds on their first date.

A Lady Specially Designed for Me

The following morning, I drove over to Sharon's apartment. We went to the market to pick up some picnic supplies. We chatted almost non-stop as we prepared sandwiches for the picnic. How comfortable she made me feel. Her gentle laugh and sense of humor began to shine through. Most of our singles showed up for the picnic, but Sharon and I stayed pretty much to ourselves as we shared glimpses of our pasts with each other. It was refreshing to walk along the beach, chatting and laughing together. It had been a long, long time since I had felt this happy and free.

At lunch time we joined the rest of the group, laid our blanket out on the sand, and ate lunch. As we were eating, one of the younger men in our group came over and attempted to cut me out by squeezing in between us. I quickly asked Sharon if she would like some dessert

She responded, "Yes."

"There are so many to choose from. Maybe you better come along so we can be certain you'll get what you like best."

She joined me. When we returned to the blanket, I sat down closer to her, leaving the younger fellow behind my back. Another young lady came by, and he wandered off with her. I had won my first "teen-age" competition contest. Of course, I had an age advantage over my competitor.

How quickly the day flew by. How much we shared our thoughts and hearts that afternoon.

On our way back to her apartment, my mood began to change. I could feel myself getting very serious about this young lady, who was almost fifteen years my junior. Was it fair to her for me to be dating her? After all, with my family history of a short lifespan, what if we did get serious about each other fell in love and married? She could become a widow at a very young age. Hadn't I told myself I would not date women more than five years younger than me? Here I was on my second date since my divorce and getting serious about her. I thought maybe I had better back away from this.

As we drove along, Sharon sensed a change in my demeanor and asked what was wrong.

"I am concerned about dating you with the difference in our ages," I replied. "I could get very serious about you."

"Why does that worry you?' she responded.

"Well, typically, my family has a very short lifespan, and I could leave you a very young widow."

"That's the strangest proposal I've ever heard," she laughed. "This is only our second date, and I didn't even know we were dating seriously."

"I'm not proposing, but I could become serious about you."

"So, what's wrong with that? It seems like I should be the one who is worried."

"I just wouldn't want to see you get hurt."

"Is it better to risk a few months or years of happiness or just go through life worrying about getting hurt or dying? Don't you believe the Lord guides us in these things?" Sharon queried.

We arrived at Sharon's door. "You're quite a lady," I responded. "If it's all right, I'll pick you up for church tomorrow."

"Sounds good to me," she said as she entered her apartment.

While driving home, I re-ran our conversation over again in my mind. I thought about her laughter when she told me we had only been out together twice, and certainly she was not thinking about love and marriage. How mature she was when she hit me right between the eyes with her very simple forthright statements. She made it clear that if love between a man and a woman is real, a difference in age is inconsequential.

What a lady, and what a mature way to look at life relationships! We were peers in so many ways. Why let arbitrary age differences block a few days, months, or years of sharing our lives? Almost from the beginning when I looked into her blue-grey eyes, I knew this was the lady the Lord had designed specially for me. Certainly she was a newer design than I had been expecting! Already she was becoming my very special lady! Of course, it was not that simple for Sharon. It took several months for the Lord to give her peace of heart and mind about me.

However, my decision had been made. I would pursue her with my whole heart. After all, isn't it better to share life with someone you love for a few months or years than to let love slip past you because you are afraid of the hurt that could come when one or the other died? So began my re-entry into the world of dating.

5 Poems

Beginning

Dinner out—our first date,
How nervously I ate.
Can he see my hands shake?
Does he hear my voice quake?

What does he think of me?
A "kindness" date? (Could be. . .)
Is he excited, too?
(Oh, how I wish I knew . . .)

I wonder if he sees
Trembling heart, trembling knees—
"Think calm"—(I can fake it.)
With God's help, I'll make it.

Does that smile mean he cares?
(Now he just sits and stares . . .)
What kind of man is this?
When will he try a kiss?

And if he tries—what then?
Will he date me again?
Lord above, help me now—
Let me feel, show me how.

You've heard my prayers at night,
Read my heart, seen my fright.
"Please, Lord, a Christian man. . .
If it be in your plan."

Why on only one date
I feel a touch of "fate"?
A feeling of rightness—
As soul lives with brightness.

Why does it scare me so?
And do I want to know?
Lord, is your hand in this?
In his touch, in his kiss?

Perhaps more time will tell—
Learning to know him well—
But why all these "guessings"
And questioning blessings?

I don't know how he feels—
What he prays when he kneels.
I'll listen hard for a clue—
(Do you like me? Do You?)

Sharon

(Written by her after our first date September 19, 1980.)

Little Bird

Small injured bird within my palm,
I hold you there without a qualm.
I feel the beating of your heart,
And long that we shall never part.

In my palm you may abide,
A shelter from life's strong tide.
Cuddle there, abide in peace,
Until from fright you find release.

My palm would close and hold you there,
Prevent your flight into the air,
To keep you here, my very own,
My soul cries out, "I can't condone!

For birds were made with wings to fly,
And soar in freedom through the sky.
Let her heal and set her free,
And she will fly right back to thee!

When she does, she'll build her nest,
With straws of love and peace and rest."
So little bird you may abide,
To heal and grow as God doth guide.

Safe in my palm,

In patient love,

Don

The Gentle Wait
Response to "Little Bird"

I am as a small injured bird,
Happy in the warmth of your palm.
Sh-h-h—do not say a word
Hold gently, stay calm . . . .

If patiently you wait,
Then when all is healed,
No way could you anticipate
The love to be revealed . . . .

Sharon

Sharon on My Mind

How close to God I feel with you,
Refreshed garden with morning dew.
The poems you write enrich my soul,
Your gentle words make me feel whole.

I look into your eyes—blue-gray,
A special message they do say,
They speak of love, also of fear,
Rest in my arms—protected dear.

Please take your time, be very sure,
My love is kind, my motives pure.
For if we have not basic trust,
Our spring of love will dry to dust.

Lives should not be like desert dry,
But soar like eagles in the sky;
And ever grow to heights above,
Be built upon undying love.

Sharon, so gentle, sweet and kind,
You are always on my mind.
My every thought of you is blessed,
And in each one is peaceful rest.

Thoughts of love,

Don

I Met a Man, Don't You See!

I'm sorry but something has happened to me,
You ask for a reason, I met a man, don't you see?
Now nothing seems to ever get done,
For he keeps me busy—we're having such fun!

Don't know if I'm better or if I am worse,
Can't even tell if he's a blessing or curse,
He loves me intensely—drives me almost insane,
That he wants to marry me, he's made very plain.

It is so very sudden, I still have my doubt,
I can't understand why he makes my heart shout,
"I love you, I love you—you're just made for me."
My mind's in a quandary; for I met a man, don't you see?

When held in his arms I feel so safe there,
Yet my mind tells me, "Move slowly—with care.
You don't really know him so why the great rush?"
But my heart says, "I love him," it's making me blush.

I'm tired of men, who will always be boys,
While I'm out there working they're playing with toys.
But this one is different—a team we will be,
Lord give assurance, I've met a man, don't you see?

To the man I met,

Love,

Sharon

Help Along Your Way – Questions for Reflection

1. What are your expectations as you consider re-entry into the dating scene?

2. What personality traits of the person you are dating would be compatible with yours?

3. What are your thoughts about future marital adjustments?

4. How can you verbalize your feelings and ideas?

5. Put into writing your feelings as you progress through a dating relationship. (Don't be concerned about your writing; just put your thoughts down.)

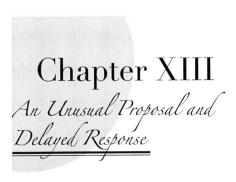

Chapter XIII
An Unusual Proposal and Delayed Response

On our fourth date, I took Sharon to see a movie. By the time I got up the courage to put my arm around her shoulder, the movie credits began. I could see a little smile cross her face. I felt very awkward at dating. We went on several dates before I kissed her. What a memorable kiss that was! The first thing she said to me following it was, "I was beginning to wonder if Baptists ever kissed." It has been a continuing point of laughter for us.

When one falls in love, it is interesting to see that person go from feeling tired and listless to being full of energy and ready to take on the world. Such was the case with me. I couldn't take her out enough. When we weren't together, I felt incomplete.

For me it was love at first sight, but not so for Sharon. I had peace that remarriage was right for me. She was still healing from her divorce and was not ready to jump back into marriage. Once again her wisdom was shining through. Too many leap back into marriage before they have worked through their grief and problems that led them into the death of a relationship. It was not so with her. After a few weeks of dating, I proposed to her. She didn't have peace about it.

Chinese Fortune Cookie Prediction

A couple of weeks later, we were dining at a Chinese restaurant. At the end of the meal, the waitress brought our check along with two Chinese fortune cookies. I opened mine and read it aloud. "You will marry your present lover and be happy." Sharon's mouth dropped open.

"You're making that up."

I showed her the fortune.

"How did you get them to do that?"

"I didn't, honest, but you better marry me or millions of Chinese are going to be heartbroken."

Part of the humor of it all was that just the night before, we had seen the movie, "Oh, God," featuring George Burns. In the movie "God" sent messages in fortune cookies. I had never gotten or seen a fortune cookie like that before, and I haven't gotten one since. Have you?

You've Garter Be Mine

At a wedding of one of Sharon's friends, I had another opportunity to propose.

All of the single men lined up to catch the bride's garter. I was obviously the oldest. A young man standing next to me said, "You may as well go and sit down, old man. I'm going to catch the garter."

I responded, "We'll have to see about that."

The groom removed the garter and tossed it into the air. The young fellow lunged for it. I gave him the hip, and as he went sprawling, I jumped and snagged it.

The young fellow was really upset and said, "That was not fair."

I smiled and quipped, "All's fair in love and war."

With a broad grin and as I twirled the garter around my finger, I again proposed. I told Sharon that all of her friends would have to wait to marry until we tied the knot. Certainly she didn't want to make them all old maids. She blushed and once again said she didn't have peace about it.

The Agapediatropha Award – Plus One

I slowly realized I was beginning to propose too often—

like a broken record. I knew I loved her and she loved me, but I had better back off. I knew she just needed space and time.

This led to a novel way of proposing without pressuring her. I decided to make it an open-ended proposal. At the time, she was working as a licensed vocational nurse (LVN) with a group of pediatricians, one of whom enjoyed acting. I contacted him to see if he would help me with my plan. I explained what I wanted to do, and he was ready and willing to help. I would give her a special humorous award.

I put together three Greek words, which I interpreted as "loving child nurse." It became the long-coveted international "Agapediatropha" award. The search began with an ancient Greek physician who searched throughout his life for the perfect child nurse. Before his death, he set up a society to continue his search. Over the centuries they had searched for this special nurse, but to no avail. Finally, the latest director of the group, Dr. Ima LuVinu, known as LVN for short, found her. Low and behold it was Sharon! I wrote a letter giving the history of the award, the centuries of searching, and the marvelous discovery.

Maggie, my secretary who also did calligraphy, was ready and willing to make the award certificate and some special coupons. The coupons included such things as dining out at the restaurant of her choice, a bicycle ride and picnic, a trip to Solvang, a day at Disneyland, etc. It included a "Plus One," which I planned to give to her that evening at a dinner I would prepare just for her.

The big day of the surprise award, I made certain she had gone to lunch. Then I took the letter, award certificate, and coupons to the doctor. After lunch, before patients arrived, he called together all of his staff to make this most prestigious award. It went off like clockwork. I think he played one of his best roles ever that day with great pomp and ceremony. Of course, halfway through the letter, Sharon sensed she had been set up.

Shortly after one o-clock, she phoned to let me know I had really gotten her good that time. Of course, by then I knew she could take a practical joke. I heard laughter in the background.

The "Plus One" really had her guessing. I told her that it would be given to her that evening at a special dinner I was preparing.

Universal Institute of Agapediatropha certificate awarded to Sharon

At the end of dinner that evening, I gave her the "Plus One" surprise. It was another certificate that read as follows: "Great for a Lifetime of Marital Bliss and Fidelity for Ms. Sharon Ryan with Donald E. Cunningham. Sign and Return to him for Satisfaction Guaranteed. Signed by Ima LuVinu." It had a signature line for her to sign when she had peace about marrying me. The pressure was off. She was free to take as much time as she wanted to find peace about her decision. Over the next few months, we relaxed and had fun as she redeemed her award coupons.

While our SPICE group was meeting in my home, we were fortunate to have Dr. Sam McDill, my Christian family and marriage counselor, volunteer to work with us. As leader of the group, I worked with Dr. Sam to set up seminars. On one such seminar, he made his large cabin in the mountains available for a weekend retreat Another couple opened their cabin so the ladies would have one totally private sleeping area and the men another.

Dr. Sam came to our group meetings for two sessions preceding the seminar. At the initial one, he outlined areas he would be covering and asked for additional suggestions. He handed out the Taylor Johnson Temperament Analysis Profiles for those planning to attend. They were to be completed by the next meeting. Sharon and I decided to do one individually and an additional one on each other. Dr. Sam agreed to this. The following week, he met with us and picked up the forms for his review and evaluation. Everyone had the opportunity to decide whether or not he or she wanted his or her profile discussed in the group meetings. Interestingly, all were willing to share.

It turned out to be a beautiful setting and a very productive, growth-supporting retreat. Dr. Sam's gracious handling of sensitive areas encouraged participants to share their experiences and concerns. In the course of the retreat, most of the group results were at the level I was when I began counseling with him.

He reserved Sharon and my profiles for his final review. His review of my profile showed me as functioning at excellent levels in all areas. What growth from a man in a dying relationship to one in love. Sharon's profile was also very positive. After reviewing each one of ours individually, he compared the ones we had completed on each other. He concluded that it was amazing how closely our assessment of each other matched our own individual evaluations. Of course, there was an ever so slight "halo" effect on our evaluations of each other. How well we had come to know ourselves and each other! I believed we were ready for marriage, but Sharon had not yet returned my proposal certificate.

A Special Birthday

Sharon was born on Christmas Eve and had never had a birthday party or a gift wrapped separately for her birthday. I decided that year would be different. A wealthy friend with whom I served on a committee invited us to go whale-watching on his yacht. It would be the day before Christmas. Sharon was hesitant to go, as her former husband had a very small sailboat he called his "yacht." There had been many unpleasant experiences related to it. The mast came loose while towing it on the freeway. Unexpected storms arose, there were wind stalls, they were soaked to the skin, and they needed to jump into cold water to pull it ashore.

When we located where the yacht was moored, we saw a beautiful three-mast ship. When we boarded it, Mike introduced us to some of his other friends and then gave us a tour. The lower cabin was solid mahogany. It had separate eating, sleeping, and bathing space as well as a full size tub. The living area had a small propane fireplace. The cabin lid had a secure water seal. The ship had a balanced keel that would right the vessel if it capsized in heavy seas. It had a large diesel engine for backup. During storms, the yacht was equipped so it could be safely guided through the waters from the weather-sealed cabin.

We sailed out of the Santa Barbara marina into the glistening waters of the Pacific. During our short journey, Mike explained to Sharon and me that he and his wife had the yacht built in order to travel around the world. Their plan was for him to retire when it was completed, and they would set sail. Shortly before its completion, his wife died. While their beautiful dreamboat was ready, his dream to sail around the world died with his wife. Now in his early eighties, he was still working and just taking short trips along the Santa Barbara coastline.

By early afternoon, we were out far enough to watch from close range a pod of whales swimming gracefully through the waves. What a breathtaking sight! Slowly the day slipped away, and we headed back toward the Santa Barbara marina.

Sharon's sailing experience turned from former negative feelings into one filled with richness and beauty. It had a close resemblance to that which was developing between us. Our previous bad experiences prior to meeting were changing to ones of love and happiness. Sharon's first birthday celebration started off with a wonderful sailing trip. Would our times together glide as gently across life's sea?

We parted long enough to clean up and prepare for our evening birthday dinner. We returned to Miramar Inn to celebrate. It was a much more relaxed time than our first date. During dinner, wrapped in birthday party paper, I gave her a gold charm necklace to which many charms would be added later. I then read her a special birthday poem I had written. She was surprised and elated with this special birthday party. The question lingered in my heart: "Was she in love with me as much as I was with her?" For now, that question remained unanswered.

The Best Christmas Present Ever!

Sharon's grandmother, Uncle Carl, and Aunt Joyce spent Christmas day with us at my mobile home. I prepared a turkey dinner with all of the fixings. I always enjoyed preparing the turkey, making a special dressing from a family recipe, and roasting it in the oven. It turned into a fun day with plenty of laughter and kidding. We exchanged gifts, poetry, thoughts, and special remembrances. I was becoming part of their family. Obviously, Sharon had close bonds with them, and they in turn had concern for her welfare, especially in the light of her divorce. Acceptance by her family was an important ingredient for our future together. Some relationships fall apart because of undermining by close relatives. Gratefully, such was not to be the case with them.

In the early evening they left for home, but the warmth of their presence lingered. Christmas was fading away. Would this be the beginning of celebrating Christmas with each other, or would it be a one-time occasion? While my heart yearned to propose again, I had committed myself to let her take all the time she needed to become comfortable with our future together. I would not go back on my word. The Lord was teaching me patience.

To get my mind off pressuring her, I sat down on the couch in front of the glowing fireplace and began to read a book Sharon had given to me. Silently, she snuggled up next to me and whispered,

"I have one more present, but I wanted to wait until we were alone to give it to you."

The flames of the fireplace reflected warmly from her face, rekindling memories of our first date. She slowly read from the paper in her hand,

"Great for a lifetime of marital bliss and fidelity…"

She handed it to me. She had signed the certificate. We were engaged! The Lord had given her peace of mind concerning her love for me. She loved me as deeply as I loved her. Oh, what a wonderful Christmas present—she loved me! The Lord knew just what kind of Christmas present I needed and had designed her especially for me. The Giver of all good gifts knew the desire of my heart and granted it to me. I felt the abundance of His grace and love. He not only put back together the broken pieces of my life, but He filled my platter with unconditional LOVE!

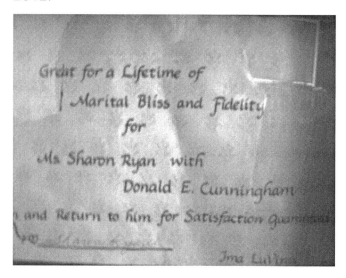

Great For a Lifetime of Marital Bliss and Fidelity
certificate signed and returned to Don

6 Poems

Sharon – My Rose

Sharon, my rose, as life unfolds,
Your clear beauty my eye beholds.
Your fragrance floats through my life's air
Bringing such sweetness—Oh, so fair.

Your body soft, so very slim
Designed and special built by Him
Enshrines a tender heart of love
And lifts me to the heights above.

The stars seem closer than before
My soul cries out, "I love you more."
Let mind conceive and heart confess
You bring undying happiness.

Your beauty like your hair is gold
I'm blessed by God, you to behold.
The deep still pools I peer into—
Your sparkling eyes of gray and blue.

Your lips so warm, so soft with charm
Speaking with love can bring no harm.
Your dainty hands with special touch
Lift up my soul so very much.

Bow drawn across a violin
Brings forth sweet music from within.
And your soft words breathed in my ear
Speak to my heart with joy and cheer.

Our arms enfold in warm caress
A token of togetherness.

Don E. Cunningham

The beauty of our first embrace
Leaves on my soul its special trace.

In Fathomless Love,

Don

Battle of the Heart
Response to Poem "Sharon – My Rose" and Rose

Oh, you were out to
win my heart
and I
to fight the giving,

The contest wasn't
fair, you see,
for love's
a need for living.

What moment was it
that you won?
when was
the tender hour?

That time of capture
of my heart
by your
poem and your flower!

Sharon

Portraits of Your Love

You painted portraits of your love,
From the great pallet of your heart.

Your mixing of your love's colors,
Is truly a work of fine art.

The sheer beauty of your portraits,
Grows in depth as the days go by,
I find it painted on my heart,
Yet can see it with my eye.

You sculpt the beauty of your love,
And etch it on my open heart.
When I hold you so close to me,
I know that we will never part.

You have done so much more for me,
Than each and every one I know.
From the time I first met you,
You have kept my heart so aglow.

Your fingers always seem to fly,
In everything I watch you do.
And in it all I see your love,
Forever it is shining through.

You're a very special person,
Whom God in love has gifted so.
I can see you use each talent,
To create such a special glow.

The presence of Christ in your life,
Shows forth His gentle spirit there.
How you have touched me with His Love,
And have lifted my every care.

So on this day of your blest birth—
I hope you know this very thing.
I will always care and love you,
Unendingly your praises sing.

Don E. Cunningham

To my Portraits of Your Love –Happy Birthday

Don

Transactional Analysis

Don,

Oh, for hours we sit and talk and discuss,
On all the important things concerning us.
Of our ideas and feelings, hopes and fears,
And what we expect from our future years.

And though we need do this, my head's been a'spin.
Oh, Eric Berne [45] , I could not hear from the din!
With my "adult" saying, "Get DATA, go slow . . ."
And my "parent"—"Watch out!" My "child"—"Let's go!"

But, wise Don Cunningham, how I do love thee—
You're willing and able to deal with all three.
You have said to my "parent"—"I will protect!
And no area of need will I neglect."

From my reasoning "adult" you've held nothing back—
Kept data banks full, so no knowledge they'd lack.
But teasing and loving and "driving me wild . . ."
Best of all, you've won over my CHILD!

Sharon

God Has Given Us Much

God has given us much since we believed,
All our frustrations and fears He relieved.

He brought us together in His great love,
Blessed by His Spirit—the Heavenly Dove.

He has given Faith and lives right inside,
He tells us, "Children in My love abide."
He has given Hope, what more could we ask?
The work we do is a heavenly task.

Blessing upon blessing He doth bestow,
Together, as one, He wants us to grow.
His Word is central and reigns in our heart,
Guides us and keeps us, through life we'll not part.

Sharon, I thank Him for all He has done,
Know through His Spirit that we will be one.
One day He will give you as my dear wife,
We'll share His bounty the rest of our life.

In His Blessed Bounty

Love,

Don

Shadow box containing courtship and wedding memorabilia

Full Cycle

I wanted to know you—

To see if I could care.

And now that I care—

I want to know you…..

Help Along Your Way – Questions for Reflection

1. How could you creatively relieve pressure if one partner is ready (and eager) to marry and the other is not?

2. What role does humor play in your courtship?

3. What ideas do the examples in this chapter give you about building a comfortable courtship?

4. What role can a professional Christian counselor play during your courtship?

5. What are some of the gifts, other than material, a couple can give to each other as they move toward marriage?

Chapter XIV
Wedding Bells Ring!

The Bell Ringers

When I was twelve years old, my father died. The rector of the Episcopal Church where my father had been sexton permitted my brother, Al, then fourteen, and me to take over as the sextons of the church. One of our duties was to ring the church bells to announce Sunday services and to toll the bells for funerals. It took both of us all our strength and ingenuity to ring them on Sunday mornings. We both would pull the rope as far down as we could. Al held the rope tightly while I jumped as high as I could and grabbed the rope. He released the rope and I flew upward. When the bell hit its highest level, the clapper fell against it. Al grabbed my legs and pulled me down and then let go. We continued doing this until the bell had been rung long enough. I then dropped down to the belfry floor. We slid down the ladder and rushed off to our Baptist Sunday school class a block away.

Tolling the bell for funerals was simpler as only one of us needed to pull the clapper against the bell. Of course, the tolling of the bell was far more solemn than the joyous ringing of the bells calling folks to worship. By the way, stories of bats in the belfry are not true. (They were in the basement; pigeons were in the belfry.)

A few months after we started working at the church, the rector told us to prepare the church for a wedding. My brother started buffing the floor, and I began dusting the pews. It suddenly dawned on me that Dr. Klein had not told us when or how to ring the bells for the wedding. I dashed through the church graveyard to his study at the rectory.

"Dr. Klein, when are we supposed to ring the wedding bells?"

He took a puff on his pipe and laughed.

"Oh, you don't ring wedding bells; they only ring in the heads of the couple getting married."

Thus began my first lesson about weddings and the ringing of wedding bells. Soon Sharon and I would hear them joyfully ringing! It would not be mournful tolling of bells in your head over the death of a relationship, but the joyous proclamation calling us to a blessed marriage.

Kissing and Telling

The morning following Sharon's acceptance of my proposal, I drove over to her apartment. I wanted her to select her own engagement ring. When we arrived at the store, she decided she would rather have both of us have nicer wedding bands. It wasn't until twenty-two years later that I was able to convince her to let me buy her an "engagement" ring. Of course, she selected it. The rings we selected bear our initials, "SMR – DEC," and "I Cor. 13." We wanted our marriage to reflect the many facets of God's love. We both knew that you don't just fall in love; you need to grow in love. How sad it is when couples fall in love, fail to nurture it, and then fall out of love.

One time I told our friends in our SPICE group that sometimes when I kissed Sharon, I would quote verses from I Corinthians 13 to myself.

"Do I love her enough to be always kind, patient, not be selfish, etc.? Do I love this lady the Lord has blessed me with to live in Godly love with her?"

How blessed a relationship can be when we reflect the many facets of God's love toward each other. How much richer all aspects of a marriage become when we embrace in love.

Of course, the guys in the group thought I was the most unromantic man they had ever seen. They could not see the

heart pounding with love in my breast. This time I would love my wife as Christ loved the church. He gave Himself for her in death. I would give myself to her in life. Years later she is still my bride, without spot or blemish!

Upon the purchase of our rings, we returned to my mobile home. We phoned both of our families to let them know we were engaged and planned to marry on Valentine's Day. All of them expressed their happiness for us. As we celebrated her birthday separate from Christmas, so would we celebrate future Valentine's Days independent from our anniversary.

We announced our engagement to our group at our New Year's Eve party and invited all of them to participate in our wedding. All of them participated in various capacities at the wedding and reception. The friend Sharon wanted to be her maid of honor had planned to go on a ski trip Valentine's weekend. She had arranged it weeks before and was hesitant to change her plans. As a joke, I bought a pair of old skis at the local thrift store, blocked them up, and ran over them with my car. Upon her arrival at our next meeting, she found the broken skis propped against my front door frame. A sign read, "Be Sharon's maid of honor or else????" When she saw it, she laughed. She said she got the message, but had already planned to reschedule her ski trip.

Be Sharon's maid of honor or else?

Do it Yourself Wedding Plans

With Sharon being an artist, we decided to decorate the church and reception hall ourselves, design our wedding invitations and thank-you notes, and prepare all of the refreshments, except for the wedding cake. Maggie, my secretary, did the calligraphy for our invitations and thank-you notes. We had them printed by a local printer. I addressed the envelopes, inserted the invitations, and mailed them out.

Our Wedding

On this day as we are wed
With our Savior as our Head,
Helping us our love to show
As we help eachother grow.

Heavenly Father, Spirit, Son,
In love uniting us as one.
Sharing all as husband ~ wife
Living daily the Christian life.

As together we embark
On our matrimonial ark,
This our prayer shall ever be,
Lord our LOVE secure in Thee.

Don & Sharon

Donald Eugene Cunningham
and
Sharon Marie Ryan
Joyously Proclaim
their
Marriage Celebration
on
Saturday, February 14, 1981
2:00 p.m.
at
Trinity Baptist Church
1002 Cienequitas
Santa Barbara, California

Reception following in fellowship hall
RSVP 805-964-6497 by February 6, 1981

Don & Sharon's Wedding Invitation

Sharon busied herself with redesigning a plain dress into a wedding gown. She also made a hand-made, flower-crested, white net veil. I wouldn't see these until our wedding day. She also made several soft sculptures, little red cupid cherubs. They would be placed on valentine hearts and crepe flowers as table decorations. Some hung from the ceiling where red and white crepe streamers crossed. In the center of the room hung a large, fold- out crepe heart. Then she created flowered crepe bows with streamers to hang on the pew ends.

Our Love Spat

Sharon had several pink and green loaves of bread baked at a local bakery. We trimmed away the crusts and cut them

into heart shapes with a cookie cutter. Then began the fun of spreading various spreads and cold cuts on them. Only a couple of days remained before the wedding bells would chime. In the midst of spreading some of the heart-shaped sandwiches with peanut butter and jam, a frown crossed Sharon's brow. I asked her what was wrong.

"It's only a couple of days until our wedding, and we haven't had our lover's quarrel yet," she responded.

"Do we have to?"

"It's always a part of the engagement ritual. I'd like to get it over with."

"Okay, then, I think we should spread the jam on the bread before the peanut butter."

"No, you always put the peanut butter on first," she countered.

"If you put the jam on first, it soaks into the bread better and makes it moister. When you flip it over, it also makes the color darker, so you have more contrast in the different sandwiches," I asserted.

"But with the bread more moist, the peanut butter won't spread as well and may tear the bread. Also, it will make peoples' hands sticky when they pick them up," she retorted.

"I think we have enough peanut butter and jam sandwiches for the reception. How about moving on to the cream cheese and olive sandwiches? Do we agree that the olives should go on top of the cream cheese?"

"It sounds good to me. What a relief to have our lovers' quarrel over with," she said with a broad grin.

Pre-Wedding Bumps

A week before our wedding, I went over to Ron and Maggie's house to help them move. Ron and I had moved several pieces of furniture into the U-haul before turning our attention to their refrigerator. We strapped it to the appliance dolly. I pulled it across the floor as Ron steadied it. I stepped backward into the garage just as the wheels of the dolly hung up on tread of the door. I gave it a heavy yank, and the dolly lunged foreword. I lost my balance, fell backward, and the refrigerator landed squarely on top of me. It held me in a full body press with my arms and legs flailing out to the sides. Ron and Maggie dashed out and came to my aid. In the panic of the moment, they imagined I would be in no shape to make it to the altar to marry Sharon the following Saturday. They lifted the refrigerator off of me. Somehow I emerged unscathed and finished loading the refrigerator into the U-Haul. The unloading went much more smoothly!

A couple of days before our wedding, Sharon and I were to meet at a local restaurant for breakfast. I was taking a couple of days off so I could get last minute things done and begin decorating the church reception hall. When she didn't arrive at the restaurant, I drove over to her apartment and knocked on her door. There was no answer. Her cousin, who would soon be moving to Israel, had recently given her his car. I decided to drive around back where she parked it. Her car was still there, but the rear window was blocked with things that she was planning to drop off at the mobile home after work.

I pulled up behind her car. As I got out, her car backed into my car. As we both looked at the damage, she began crying and asked, "Does this mean the wedding is off?"

"No, it just means I have to add a visit to the body shop to see how much it will cost for repairs," I laughed.

Maggie and Ron Thompson with Jane Galbraith at wedding pointing at dented fender on Don's Pinto

It was too late to have breakfast together, so she scurried off to work. I added the body shop to my list of things to do. The body shop gave a very reasonable estimate and set a date when I could bring it in for repairs. I phoned Sharon to let her know the outcome and that the price was reasonable enough to not file a claim. After that, I went over to the church and began decorating the reception hall. I quit early enough to prepare a surprise dinner for Sharon. I figured she would enjoy a relaxing meal after the stresses of the day.

SPICE Group's Wedding Rehearsal Dinner.

The night of our wedding rehearsal, Sharon's Aunt Joyce and Uncle Carl took us out for an early dinner. They had helped raise Sharon and were like parents to her. Uncle Carl would be giving Sharon away. The light dinner was followed by a trip to church for the wedding rehearsal. Ron and Wilna were there. You will remember them from my Love Cave experience. He was my best man in every sense of the word. Also, another dear pastor and his wife were there. He would be participating in the marriage ceremony.

The rehearsal went well with lots of lighthearted laughter. All of our friends in our SPICE group were there and enjoying their roles in the big event. They told us previously that they wanted to provide the wedding rehearsal dinner. What a dinner it was!

Following the rehearsal, we went over to Peggy's house for dinner. The group had the buffet table gala decorated and loaded with tons of food. Peggy had an electronic organ in her home. Uncle Carl had taught himself to play the organ and had a similar one in his family room. Following dinner, he sat down and began to play it. The group gathered around him, requesting he play their favorite songs and hymns. It turned into an evening of song and laughter. The prelude to our marriage could not have been any more wonderful!

Police Intervention

Early in the morning on our wedding day, I took the sandwiches, nuts, mints, punch, and other goodies over to the church reception hall to have everything ready. I unlocked the door and took every thing inside. To be certain everything was in order in the sanctuary, I decided to go in and check it out. I returned to the reception hall and began putting the sandwiches in the refrigerator. I heard the door bang open.

"Come out with your hands raised."

I raised my hands and turned to see two policemen with their guns pointed toward me.

"What are you doing in here at this hour of the morning?"

"I'm setting things up for my wedding."

"You don't look like you're dressed for a wedding. Besides, the silent alarm came from the sanctuary, not this section of the building."

"I was just checking to see if everything was in place there. I didn't know there was a silent alarm in there."

"That's the purpose of a silent alarm."

At that point our pastor came in, identified himself, and told them he had received a call from the alarm company. He said he hadn't expected me to get to the church before him. He had forgotten to mention to me that there was a silent alarm and that I should wait until after 8 a.m. before entering the church. I gave the officers some sandwiches and apologized for the inconvenience. They were the first to partake of the food from our reception. They left with their usual comment, "Have a nice day!" I knew the rest of the day would be exciting in a much more positive way.

The Wedding Bells Ring

Once I had everything in order, I returned home to clean up and get dressed for our day of blessing. How bountiful those blessings were. Our singles' group saw that everything went as smoothly as a well-catered wedding. Tom, our baritone soloist, had once sung in the Metropolitan Opera House. For years he sang in First-mate Bob's male quartet. His rendition of the Lord's Prayer still rings in our hearts. Our pastor's wife assisted at the organ. Tears came to my eyes as I heard the wedding march begin and saw my beautiful bride, without spot or blemish, coming toward me. Her Uncle Carl had a broad smile across his face as he walked beside her. The wedding went smoother than rehearsed. I heard those wonderful words, "You may kiss your bride." When I started to kiss her a second time, the pastor quipped, "Only one for now, Don."

When we turned to walk together down the aisle, we saw Sharon's cousin sitting on the front seat crying. He was like a brother to her. Just days before, he had started his lonely walk through the valley of the shadow of divorce. It was a reminder of where we had been. Later, in privacy, Sharon was able to console him and let him know we would be there for him.

The reception was a festive occasion with all of the bride and groom rituals. Sharon's dearest friend, Marilyn, caught the bridal bouquet. For many years she stood by Sharon through thick and thin. A short time after catching the bouquet, she met her dream man and married.

Don and Sharon cutting wedding cake –
He makes all things beautiful

Laughter and food abounded. Many heartfelt wishes were exchanged. In the midst of the celebration, Sharon's tiny eighty-year-old grandmother told me she wanted to talk to me outside. She held me by the wrist as she led me toward the door. Once outside, she leaned on her cane with one hand; with the other, she pointed her finger, threateningly, in my face. She looked me squarely in the eyes and said, "Don, I know you say you love Sharon, but if you ever do the least little thing to hurt her, I will come up to Santa Barbara and kick your butt all around this town." Gram let me know how much she loved our Sharon. She need never worry about our relationship. Had not our Lord designed Sharon especially for me? He had used Gram, Aunt Joyce, Uncle Carl, and her mother as subcontractors in the process.

A few months later, when we were visiting Gram's, she took Sharon aside and told her, "Sharon, you've got a good man there. Treat him right or I'll kick your butt all around Santa Barbara." What unbiased love she had for each of us!

2 Poems

Sharing and Caring

What will it be like after that wonderful day,
When we walk down the aisle and start on our way?
What kind of joy and peace will be deep in our hearts,
When we've united as one our two separate parts?

The old scars of the past must be well understood,
So that they can heal and really work for our good.
If they hurt us when the storms of life we must face,
Pain will remind each of us to exercise grace.

To support one another as we have growing pains,
Through our experiences we'll show marriage gains.
To actively listen when our hearts we must bare,
And give reassurance that we really care.

When tensions arise as they assuredly will,
To look at the causes with our love and our skill;
God's Word will set the standards and will be our guide,
With our love and affection, be gently applied.

We promise each other and our Great God of love,
We will pray and seek guidance through the Holy Dove;
To walk with each other hand and hand throughout life,
We'll be sharing and caring as husband and wife.

Caring while waiting to be sharing,

Love,

Don

Open Heart

Don –

So much love you give me, so wide open and free,
Oh, so open your heart is when you look at me.
There are times I've looked away so you wouldn't know
Just how deeply I cared, how you've made my love grow.

Or how much I longed to give it all, without stop,
For my love overflows—it is filled to the top.
So much energy it takes to stay in control—
To release love slowly when I want to give the whole.

I guess I've been cautious and so afraid of pain,
Afraid of our hurting if our love should wane.
In not wanting to make another mistake,
I've sought restraints for my heart, for both our sake.

But then when I've seen you so fearlessly giving
And, loving me, making me glad to be living—
How can I do anything but give all I am?
Follow your lead; offer the whole—every last dram.

If there's hurt then so be it, God knows my fate,
Here my love comes a-flooding—you've opened the gate!

Sharon

Help Along Your Way – Questions for Reflection

1. What facets of God's love do you want to shine in your marriage? (See I Corinthians 13.)

2. What are the fun things you are doing, as a couple, to plan your wedding and honeymoon?

3. How are you learning to verbalize your feelings and ideas with your prospective mate?

4. How do you plan to involve other divorced singles and friends in your wedding service?

5. When "bumps" occur in your wedding plans, how will you handle them—tragedy or comedy?

Chapter XV
You Mean I Can't Lead Lord, Or Can I?

While our divorced singles' group, SPICE, which I started in my home, was sanctioned by our pastor, I was troubled that this was the only area in which I was permitted to serve.

Over the years I had been a pastor, teacher, Sunday school superintendent, chairman of the deacon board, church moderator, and chairman of many other church committees. Now, because I was divorced, none of these leadership opportunities appeared to be available to me.

When a Christian service questionnaire was passed out in church, I listed my background and volunteered to teach adults. Even though they later announced a need for teachers, I was not called.

The following year I once again filled in a similar questionnaire, attached a resumé, and volunteered to be a substitute teacher. One understanding college professor friend asked me to teach his class one week, "just to see how the church would respond."

The class responded very well and gave positive feedback to him. He was later told by the chairman of the deacon board that I was not "qualified" to teach. He didn't define for him what he meant by "qualified." While I had two college degrees with a Bible theology and pastoral emphasis; taught teacher training in former churches; and had a life-time teaching credential at the California junior college level, I did not challenge the deacon. The answer was clear that while I was "qualified" to lead a group of divorced singles in my home, I was not "qualified" to teach in the church.

Following a presentation by the general director of our state organization outlining the pressing need for pastors, Sharon and I discussed the possibility of returning to a pastoral ministry. I contacted the general director, completed a multi-page application, attached a resumé, and sent it to him. I followed this up with a phone call contact. A short time later, Sharon and I met with him. While he was supportive, he told us honestly that as I had been divorced and remarried, it was doubtful any church would call us. He was the first church official to tell me that, as a divorced person, I could not lead. I appreciated his upfront honesty.

The pastor who supported our SPICE group retired, and a new young pastor was called. About six months after his arrival, I gave him a copy of my application and resume and told him of my desire to serve as a minister of pastoral care. I outlined for him my thinking regarding that area of ministry. I told him if he felt my divorce and remarriage would disqualify me, I would understand. He said he would review my application and think about it. I heard nothing further from him. The church's passive silence was more deadly to me than a simple "no." I could have accepted an explanation, based on scriptural grounds that I could not serve in a leadership position.

Here, as in other areas of my walk through the valley of the shadow of divorce, the Lord didn't want me to have an easy "yes" or "no" answer from church leadership. He clearly wanted me to pound it out upon the anvil of my heart.

I Timothy 3:2 & 12 instructs us:

"A bishop then must be blameless, the
husband of one wife, temperate, sober-minded,
of good behavior, hospitable, able to teach…….
Let deacons be husbands of one wife, ruling their
children and their own houses well." [46]

Anyone wanting to be a leader in the church must review

that position in the context of I Timothy 3. To be honest, it must be viewed not only from "a husband of one wife" perspective, but from all of the criteria outlined by Paul. The church must also address the fact that this text does not make a distinction between widowed or divorced men who take a second wife. On the one hand, I have seen remarried widowers serve on conservative church boards. On the other hand, divorced and remarried divorced men have been excluded. Another irony is that in some instances where remarried divorced men relocate and do not mention their prior divorce, they are accepted to serve. It is evident that inconsistencies exist from church to church.

Another approach taken by some churches is that in Paul's day, polygamy was common, and what he really meant was, "the husband of one wife at any one time." During the earlier years of my remarriage, I had difficulty accepting this interpretation. In later years it would become more acceptable. I continued to seek the Lord's answer to my question: "Does this mean I can't lead, Lord?"

His answer for the time being appeared to be, "Yes, Don, at this time and in this place, it means you can't lead. Just continue to serve me."

Thank the Lord; He can always use us as His servants. As I looked back over my life, I saw this as a reconfirmation of the truth He sealed to my heart several years before when He lead me out of the pastoral ministry and into a ministry in social work. That, too, was a time of heartbreaking self-examination. The end result of both of these personal encounters with the Lord and His Word is that even though leadership in the church may not be possible, service to the Lord in my daily walk can be a reality.

Sharon and I continued to serve with our SPICE group and attend church services. One day, while attending the wedding of my best friend's oldest daughter, his wife, Wilna, approached me to see if I would retire from my program coordinator position and come to work for Ron. Later in the day he raised the same question. In all the years I knew him, I never saw him looking so weary. I told them I would pray about it and let them know. We had two other factors to consider in making our decision. Sharon's grandmother was displaying symptoms of Alzheimer's disease, and her Uncle Carl was disabled by a stroke. We needed to be closer to them to help with their care and supervision. After much prayer and discussion, Sharon and I decided to accept Ron and Wilna's offer. I resigned my position, and we moved to Riverside, California.

Or Maybe I Can!

We found a new church home and began attending regularly. The pastor, while conservative in his theology, was active in social issues. Over a period of months we formed a positive bond. He asked me if I would teach a Wednesday night class. It would be made up of adults who were having social adjustment struggles. I obtained Dr. Sam McDill's permission to use his Scripturally based book, *The Master's Design for Discovering Your "Self."* I learned from a third party that the deacon overseeing Christian education was opposed to my teaching a class. He did not make an issue of it.

The class started off slowly, but grew throughout the four months. The interaction was stimulating, and the group gradually adjusted to one another. I saw individual growth developing in the class members. Several friendships were formed. At the end of the final class, evaluation forms were completed and turned in. All of those attending the class indicated personal growth and a desire for the class to continue the following year. It was exhilarating to be teaching again!

During the months I was teaching, one major change took place in our church. Our beloved pastor resigned to continue his education toward becoming a university sociology professor. A new pastor was called who was very conservative and not interested in social action issues. Needless to say, I was not asked to teach the class, and it was dropped from the curriculum. Over a period of months, most of the young adults who attended my class moved on to other churches. Sharon and I were isolated in a church we had grown to love.

Upon my retirement, Sharon and I moved to Prescott Valley, Arizona. We began attending a small Baptist church. A very young, untrained pastor had just become minister of the church. Sharon and I were asked to co-teach a Sunday school class of fifth and sixth graders. Sharon took the lead in the class, and I added supportive insights. She also became active with the young children's Monday evening group.

A few months after our arrival, several leading members of the church became disgruntled with the young pastor. A church meeting was called to fire him. The leaders brought in several members who had moved from the area but were still on the church rolls. They succeeded, by a narrow margin, in unseating the pastor. Sharon and I decided we could not accept the tactics used by the board and began seeking a new church home.

After visiting several local churches, we made a major denominational change from Baptist to Methodist. We came to love our new pastor. He had been raised in fundamental Methodist and Baptist churches. A few months after joining the church, a remarkable turning point came in our lives.

I was working part-time for a local contractor. I did all of the little touch-up jobs preceding the homeowner's final inspection. I was also on call to fix minor problems homeowners had after moving into their homes. During my younger years, as a janitor, I developed the pattern of praying while cleaning buildings. I called it "dust mop devotions." One day, as I was sweeping out a duplex and having devotions, I suddenly began crying. I was still grieving my inability to use the gifts I so desired to use in service to my Lord. Finally, I burst out: "Lord, you know my heart. You gave me gifts to use in Your service, which are lying dormant. If it is Your will that I serve you by sweeping floors, then I submit to Your will."

While the tears continued to flow, a warm, gentle peace flowed through my heart. Peace at last! When I arrived home, Sharon knew instantly that something had happened. I couldn't speak, but I fell into her arms and began crying. After a few moments, I was able to tell her what happened during my devotions. We cried together.

That afternoon, Pastor Terry Reid stopped by for a visit. We chatted for a little while then he asked, "Don, would you consider becoming our minister of pastoral care and outreach?"

Sharon and I were stunned. We looked at one another, and tears began to flow.

Pastor Terry looked surprised and blurted out, "Did I say something wrong?"

"No, you just gave us the Lord's answer to years of prayer."

We explained to him what I had experienced that morning. Terry assured us that God's grace was sufficient in all areas of our lives including ministry. Finally, the Lord had said, "Yes, Don, you can lead!"

After almost twenty years of struggling with the desire to minister in His church, the Lord had opened the door of opportunity to me. What a joyous ministry awaited me! I could serve my Lord as lay minister of pastoral care in the church and be His representative in our community.

From my experience in various churches over the years, there appears to be no clear position concerning divorced and remarried individuals as it relates to leadership positions in the church. Some authors have attempted to outline what positions should be available to these individuals. Yet many churches and pastors avoid confronting the issue by silence on the subject. Depending on the perspective of individual pastors and church boards, a divorced and remarried person may or may not be allowed to serve in leadership positions. The position may be totally reversed with a pastoral change in the same church.

A divorced and remarried individual convinced that she/he is scripturally qualified to assume a leadership position in the church should discuss it openly with the pastor.

Regardless of the decision, the individual can serve our Lord as a servant to others. Certainly, as we have grown through divorce, our service and support of others walking through the valley of the shadow of divorce is a viable and rewarding experience. Whether one is permitted to lead or not, all are called to be servants and can serve.

Help Along Your Way – Questions for Reflection

1. Who in your church leadership do you feel comfortable with discussing your role in the church?

2. How does your church view divorced/remarried members as it relates to leadership roles?

3. What opportunities do you have to use your gifts inside and outside your church?

4. Have you considered moving to a church that will allow you to use your gifts?

5. How do you exercise the role of servant in your community?

Chapter XVI
Remarriage Beautiful All the Time

Our First Year Together

There would be two phases to our honeymoon. We would spend one week along the coast near San Luis Obispo. In the fall we planned a trip back home to Troy, New York, to visit with my family, who were anxious to meet Sharon.

The week near San Luis Obispo was all a couple could anticipate on a honeymoon. We shared our love in a beautiful honeymoon suite overlooking the Pacific Ocean. Two of the seven nights were paid for by dear friends. We strolled along the beach, swam, and enjoyed a hot tub. There were several excellent restaurants nearby to which friends at work and in our singles' group had given us gift certificates. For a couple in love, it could not have been a more beautiful or romantic setting. What a wonderful beginning on our journey through life together!

A couple of months following our wedding, I was up in that area on agency business. On my lunch hour, I decided to wander through the J.C. Penney store. I saw a double-switch electric blanket at 70% off. The temptation was too great—I bought it. At our next divorced singles' meeting when prayer requests were being taken, Sharon asked that the group pray for our marriage as she thought it was in trouble. Everyone looked shocked, including me. The prayer leader hesitantly asked what was wrong. "I guess Don thinks I can't keep him warm anymore. He bought a double-switch electric blanket." The group erupted into laughter. (That was the last electric blanket I bought.)

In the fall, we flew back to Troy, New York, to spend time with my family. As a joke, before we left, I bought my Southern California bride a pair of long-johns. It turned out that she wore them all the time we were back there. One day, we sat on my brother's side porch. We were enjoying the fall colors when my brother mentioned what a beautiful Indian summer day it was. Sharon responded, "But you can see your breath." My bride was learning what an upstate New York fall was like. Of course, my family fell in love with her.

On our wedding day, I gave Sharon a gold necklace and a specially handcrafted cross with intertwined hearts on it. A couple of weeks before our trip back home; she was having upper-back pain so the doctor ordered an x-ray. While she was having the x-ray taken, someone opened the locker in which she had placed her clothing and necklace. When she was getting dressed, she discovered that the necklace and cross had been stolen! Staff claimed that no one had been near the locker. I returned to the jeweler to see if he could make a cross out of my old wedding band. He told me that because it was a combination of yellow and white gold he could not do so.

I remembered that one of my former high school classmates was a goldsmith. I took my old wedding band with me on our trip to see if he could make a cross with intertwined hearts out of it. He studied it carefully and said it would be tricky, but that he would be willing to try fashioning it. He said he would also put golden intertwined hearts on it. A few days later, imagine Sharon's surprise when I placed a new necklace with the cross and hearts dangling from it around her neck. Tears of joy flowed down her face. The band that had bound me was now a symbol of God's eternal love with two hearts joined together forever!

*Don's old wedding band made into cross with two
gold entwined hearts on it*

While back there, we took several day trips into New England, enjoying the changing foliage and the many art and historical museums in the area. The second half of our honeymoon was as blessed as the first, only in an entirely different setting. Sharon especially enjoyed our trip to Lake George and Lake Champlain. Their size, beauty, and history left a lasting imprint on her. The beautiful Berkshire, Adirondack, and Catskill Mountains were ablaze with their wide array of brightly colored leaves. It seemed as if all nature was applauding our union. Our flight home over the bright fall foliage was equally inspiring.

One afternoon, about ten months after our marriage, Sharon came home from the market. I could tell by the downcast look on her face that something had upset her. I asked her what was wrong, and she burst into tears. I held her for a few moments. The tears stopped, and she said she had seen our pastor. He asked her if we had had our first argument yet. When she said, "No," he told her that if we hadn't argued yet our marriage wasn't normal. It crushed her.

I told her that it is the norm for most couples to argue, so it was obvious that our marriage was not normal. It was above the norm, making it more beautiful. A broad smile crossed her face. Twenty-five years later, it is still above the norm!

On the first anniversary of our marriage, we sent a poem to all of our friends who had attended our wedding. It follows:

First Anniversary Thanksgiving

It was only a year ago,
Seeds of marriage you saw us sow.
Dear friends we write that all is well,
We together in God's love dwell.

The beauty of our hearts entwined,
So permeates our souls and mind.
We've had a year to love and grow,
Hearts of each other come to know.

Our love has grown as we have shared,
The tender touch that showed we cared.
And as we talk or sit and read,
We meet each other's inward need.

Trials have come in this blessed year,
Drawn us together—held us near.
Our lives blended in wedded bliss,
Together chat and share a kiss.

Sometimes we sit and pray and praise,
In thanksgiving our voices raise.
We thank our Lord for His great love,
Shared each day through the Holy Dove.

They say this is the paper year,
And so we write to friends so dear,
Saying our love has grown with zest,
And that the Lord our marriage blest.

With Love,

Don and Sharon Cunningham

Maturing Love

In his book, *Growing in Remarriage*, Jim Smoke devotes a chapter to "The Seasons of Marriage." [47] It illustrates the stages of remarriage growth through the four seasons of the year. The seeds of love Sharon and I had sown in the spring of our courtship and marriage had taken root. Summer had warmed and nurtured them into strong, growing plants. We had the beauty of flowers all around us. The vegetables and fruits that would nourish our marriage were growing toward the harvest of an abundant life together. There were none of the bugs or weeds in our relationship that sometimes plague remarried couples. While there were some health trials trying to take root, we were enjoying our marital bliss.

Over the ensuing ten years of our marriage, we began to harvest the fruits of our love labors together. My two sons had their own families and fully accepted Sharon. We did not face the stresses of raising younger children in our remarriage. Several other family stresses would test our relationship. Rather than creating tensions between us, they brought us together in an even greater bond of love. Ours would be the challenge and blessing of caring for an elderly grandmother, aunt, and uncle. With an aging population, I believe this will become more and more a factor in remarriages.

The second Christmas following our marriage, Sharon's Uncle Carl was disabled by a stroke. Her Aunt Joyce decided that she would care for him at home. We began helping her keep their affairs in order and coordinate medical services for him. Occasionally, things in their home would break down, and I would replace them. Everything Uncle Carl had installed in their home had written on them the installation dates and where he had filed the manuals. All of his files were clearly organized, making it much easier to manage things.

Even though he was wheelchair-bound and unable to care for himself, he maintained a marvelous sense of humor. He loved to have me tell him jokes and relate humorous things that had occurred over the years. He gestured with his good hand to encourage me to tell him more. It was heart-wrenching to see a beautiful mind only able to express itself with the movement of a hand, a grunting noise, a slight headshake, and a broad smile.

For twelve years Joyce cared for him at home. She took him for therapy, occasional day care, short visits with us, and to the doctors. She hired a student nurse to come in once a week so she could do the marketing. As she aged and his needs increased, I contacted his doctor to attempt to arrange for some in-home health care. He refused, saying Carl needed to be in a nursing home. He was too great a burden on Joyce. I told him that was Joyce's decision and she wanted him at home. He said he would not authorize in-home health care and hung up. I immediately contacted the local Visiting Nurses Association, explained the situation, and requested an in-home evaluation. An evaluation was done, and the services were authorized. In less than a month, Uncle Carl died in his sleep. How much more traumatic it would have been for Joyce if we had followed the doctor's advice and placed him in a nursing home! The Lord had blessed our joint decision. I participated in the memorial service to celebrate Uncle Carl's life.

Shortly after our marriage, Sharon's grandmother asked me if I would handle her affairs when the time came that she could no longer make her own decisions. Before agreeing to do so, we sat down with her to discuss exactly how she wanted things done. We covered areas of finances, assistance with living arrangements, if needed, and her memorial service. She made it very clear that she did not want to place an additional burden upon us by coming to live in our home. When the time came, she wanted to be sure I placed her in a nice "home." Her sense of humor came through when we discussed planning her memorial service. When I suggested a couple of pastors in the area, she responded with, "You do my funeral service. You know me. I don't want any preacher saying nice things about me that might not be true!" I would follow her wishes in all of these areas. Grams had thoroughly accepted me and would not be "kicking my butt all around Santa Barbara."

When she was about eighty-eight years old, she was diagnosed with Alzheimer's disease. We were able to arrange for a person to provide in-home care for the first year after her diagnosis. At that point, because of her increased needs, I placed her in an assisted-living program. Her grandmother's mental decline to the point where she no longer recognized Sharon was crushing. Her care needs increased beyond the large facility's ability to meet them. We found a small family care home operated by a nurse. The loving care she received was beyond anything we could have provided in our home. At ninety-five, her medical needs increased to the point that I had to move her to a nursing home. She died two weeks after the move. Her death came a little over a year after Uncle Carl's. As promised, I conducted her memorial service.

The stress of managing the affairs of three families would have been unendurable had it not been for the tight bond of love Sharon and I had for each other. Seeing the loved ones who had helped raise her from early childhood slowly slipping away was very difficult for Sharon. In the midst of all this, on our ninth anniversary, I wrote the following poem:

A Cat Has Nine Lives

Happy Ninth Anniversary

They say a cat has nine lives,
I don't know if that is true.
I know that God gives one life,
To folks like me and you.

But within His loving heart,
The two of us made one.
His love that grows within us,
Is work that is not done.

It has grown and truly blossomed,
With the splendor of a rose.

In our nine years of marriage,
We know it grows and grows.

You are so very special,
In all you say and are.
With the eyes of love I see you,
You're without a spot or mar.

Oh, my darling how I love you,
I thank our special Lord,
That blessing upon blessing,
Upon our lives He poured.

Now on our anniversary,
These words to you I say,
My darling how I love you,
Every day in every way.

Love,

Don

Years of Untarnished Gold

As we prepared for retirement, we visited areas in New Mexico and Arizona. We chose the town of Prescott Valley, Arizona, as the place where we would spend our retirement years. Uncle Carl had died, and we invited Aunt Joyce to come live with us. Initially, she rejected the idea, so we bought a nice, single-family home. Shortly after our move, she decided that she wanted to live with us. For almost a year we went through the frustration of working with contractors to build an addition to our home. Once completed, it took Aunt Joyce several months to place her home on the market and sell it. Then came the long Labor Day week when we went to help her finish getting ready for her move. Though several months had passed,

Joyce could not bring herself to do any packing. We spent four extremely hectic days, cleaning out a fifty-year accumulation in her garage, storage shed, and house. This was combined with a garage and yard sale. On Labor Day, I struck my head on a two-by-four and spent several hours in the emergency room waiting for the gash to be sewed up.

The moving van arrived a day early, adding to the stress. We survived the ordeal and had Joyce safely moved. Due to her age, we made the addition fully wheelchair accessible. By that time I had assumed responsibility for all of her financial affairs. It seemed that each additional area of stress and responsibility drew Sharon and me closer together.

During that time, I had the joy of serving as lay minister of pastoral care and with several non-profit groups in our community. Sharon supported me in all of these areas. As I approached my seventieth birthday, health problems increased. I was diagnosed with asthma. I slowly withdrew from many of my activities. In my seventy-first year, I required quadruple-bypass surgery and several other surgeries. After several sinus surgeries, I lost my sense of smell.

The day following my return home from my heart surgery, a heavy hail and rainstorm struck our area. Sharon was taking care of me and didn't go down to her art studio until four days later. It was flooded, and mold had begun to form on the walls. It wasn't until she had worked down there for three more months that we learned how deadly the mold was. One Sunday she saw an article about a family in Texas whose home contained stachybotrus mold. Several of the symptoms the family was having matched ours. Some of our symptoms were spontaneous bruising, headaches, asthma attacks, body pain, shortness of breath, short-term memory loss, and sinus infections. The deadly stachybotrus spores attack the central nervous and immune systems. I cut a patch out of the wall and took it to a lab. It was the deadly mold. By now it had gotten into our air system and spread throughout the house. We had to hire a bio-hazard team to rip out walls and clean the entire air system. We had to dispose of all porous materials including drapes, furnishings, carpet, etc. At the same time, we had a mouse infestation in our basement, which required even more work on our home.

For two years, every week, and sometimes more often, we took a two hundred mile roundtrip to an environmental health specialist for detoxification treatments. We still have not completely recovered from its devastating effects upon our immune and central nervous systems.

It seems that in our twenty-five years of a wonderful marriage, we have figuratively faced the "Plagues of Egypt." Everything that has buffeted us from without has only strengthened our relationship.

In the midst of the ordeals, we had one of our most memorable anniversary celebrations. We made reservations for the private room at our favorite Indian restaurant, The Guru. We had become close friends with the owner and his family. The little intimate room would be ours for the evening. We sat on pillows in the candle-lit room. Gentle music played in the background. Roses, surrounded by candles, graced the short table. Between the courses, we reminisced about our marriage by reading poetry we had written to each other over the years. The soft, warm glow of a mature love flickered in our eyes as we shared intimate moments together. How the precious memories lingered in our hearts and minds.

For twenty-five years our love for one another has grown. When we have had differing viewpoints, we have always been able to discuss our perspectives and arrive at a solution. Usually, her insights have prevailed.

In this area, I often think of an episode we had when taking my grandsons for a ride. After making some ridiculous statement, I asked,

"Isn't that right, John?"

He responded, "No, Grandpa, it isn't."

I replied, "If Grandpa isn't right, who is then?"

"Sharon."

"When is she right?'

Then he gave this pearl of wisdom: "All the time!"

Over the last twenty-five years, I found his little pearl of

wisdom to be very accurate. Sharon has never spoken an angry or unkind word to me. She continues to be my "bride without spot or blemish."

Two months before Sharon found the peace to accept my proposal, I wrote the following poem. I knew in my heart she would marry me. It has been the pattern we have followed throughout our marriage.

Holy Spirit, Lead

Please, Holy Spirit, flow through us,
And may we never fume and fuss;
Walk ever in the Christian life,
As always loving husband—wife.

Holy Spirit, guide every step,
That we in love be ever kept.
To walk together side by side,
With You always our precious guide.

Holy Spirit, rule in our hearts,
Bring together the separate parts.
In our marriage two live as one.
Through love of Father-Spirit-Son.

Holy Spirit, wed in Your Word,
Add to our lives as it is heard.
Help us to live it every day,
As we walk on our pilgrim way.

Holy Spirit, do us baptize,
As we gaze in each other's eyes.
Let us see our dear Father's love,
And know He rules us from above.

Holy Spirit, give us courage,
In love the other one nourish,

That each of us may grow in grace,
Until we see Thee face to face.

Holy Spirit, help us to learn,
And on our hearts Your wisdom burn.
Your Love and Faith and Hope impart,

That we may share our Savior's heart.
Holy Spirit, we now thank You,
That together our hearts you woo.
Sharing, Loving with heart and mind.
May our lives be sweetly entwined.

As the Spirit leads

Love

Don

Don & Sharon Cunningham

Married February 14, 1981

Santa Barbara, California

Twenty Year Princess

Down the aisle comes my precious bride,
Makes my heart leap with joy and pride.
For twenty years our love has grown,
You're the PRINCESS on my heart's throne.
I thank the Lord for you each day,
You've made me PRINCE in every way!

Published in *The Daily Courier*, Prescott, AZ
On our twentieth wedding anniversary.

LOVE,
Don

Our Silver Bells Ring

Our silver bells are ringing clear,
They tell of all that we hold dear.
Twenty-five years of precious love,
Bountiful blessings from above!

Our happiness the day we wed,
Throughout our marriage has been spread.
The frosting on our cake was sweet,
But with our Love it can't compete.

Twenty-five years, our love has grown,
How glad we are the seed was sown.
So many joys that we have reaped.
Blessings on blessings have been heaped.

Many joys and stresses we've known,
And through it all our love has shone.
Aging comes—illness follows fast,
But through it all our love will last.

Thank you Lord for our Precious Love,
Your bounty to us from above.
Our years of marriage you have blest,
Helped love to grow through every test.

The silver bells joyously ring,
Our message clear to all they bring.
We say to all the good news spread,
We're thankful for the day we wed.

**HUGS, IN CHRIST'S AND OUR LOVE
ON OUR TWENTY-FIFTH WEDDING ANNIVERSARY**

Help Along Your Way – Questions for Reflection

1. What adjustments do you anticipate you will need to make during your first year of marriage?

2. In what ways do you want your marriage to be normal? Above normal?

3. What will you include in your first anniversary poem or note to family and friends?

4. What experiences in your marriage do you believe will help mature your love toward each other?

5. How do you plan to turn negative events impacting your lives into positive marriage growth experiences?

Chapter XVII
We Plan for the Future

I jokingly refer to our marriage as a spring-winter relationship. I was born in early May, and Sharon was born in late December. In reality, when we married, she was in the summer bloom of life, and I was in the mid-autumn of my days. My grey hair symbolized the nipping frost of fall, but it had a nice "puff" to it! The "puff" resulted in one of my co-workers giving me the endearing and enduring nickname of "puff head."

As I mentioned in an earlier chapter, my family history shows a very short adult life span. My father died in his early forties. A sister died of influenza when only a year old. My oldest brother died in his early fifties. Two weeks after my wedding, my other sister died in her mid-fifties. Another brother passed away a couple of years later in his early fifties. With the exception of my toddler sister, all the members of my family died of heart attacks. This made me keenly aware of my responsibility toward Sharon and her future.

The way I view my bride is very different from that of some older men who see their younger brides as trophies and below their level of maturity and intelligence. Sharon, while beautiful both in body and spirit, is my cherished gift from God. Ours was a match made in Sunday school and designed in Heaven!

We are compatible with each other and share a spirit of mutual respect. Intellectually and educationally we are at very similar levels. In some areas, she displays a better balance of maturity than I do. We enjoy similar things such as reading, writing poetry, attending church, art, plays, and just plain being together. Just enjoying one another's presence may not sound that important for a strong marriage. In reality, it is core! Hugs and kisses occur at the most unexpected moments. Whether demonstrated in word or deed, a simple "I love you" during the day helps keep our relationship alive and vital.

When we first married, it didn't seem that our love could be any richer. Yet over the years it has grown much deeper. External pressures have welded our spirits into a unified bond of love and understanding. We have become one in Christ.

A Will to Live

While prenuptial agreements and protection of assets are important in some second marriages, our income and assets were not that significant. A few weeks after our wedding, I began talking to Sharon about the importance of a will and renaming beneficiaries on my insurance policies. She was reluctant to discuss these areas for two reasons. First, she felt that my sons should continue as my beneficiaries. I viewed our primary responsibilities to be toward each other. The second feeling was the reason many couples do not do long range planning. They do not want to discuss the issues of death.

At first, Sharon thought I was focusing too much on my "impending death." Over the years, this has given occasion for her to kid me. Sometimes, when we are discussing long range planning, she comments with a sly smile, "But you promised to leave me a young widow." How thankful we are for the special years we have shared together with relatively good health.

When Sharon saw how important this area was to me, she consented to having a new will drawn up. An attorney friend, a former associate with me in social work, met with us to draw up the will. He made it clear to Sharon that she was free to have another attorney work on her behalf. She decided that he could draw up both of our wills. After reviewing my part of the will, he began discussing with Sharon which persons she wanted to include in hers. She said she would like to name me first, and then my sons as her beneficiaries. When I told her she didn't need to name my sons in her will, she looked hurt and respond-

ed, "Don't you know I love them as much as you do?" That is the only time I have seen a tear trickle down an attorney's face. What a gracious lady I had married!

Then there are those marriage situations where the older man has decided that he has been active long enough and just wants to retire and take life easy. During the first twenty years of our marriage, Sharon had difficulty keeping up with me physically. We enjoyed many activities. We had fun traveling on vacations. We took walks in the evening. She enjoyed stopping to smell the roses, while I looked at the construction of buildings. Now that I have no sense of smell, I wish I had stopped to smell the roses a little more often.

While on a weekend trip to San Diego with our dearest friends, Ron and Wil, we decided to look at some new condos. The three of them were enjoying the ocean views. I took a brief look and began checking out the horsepower of the garbage disposal under the kitchen sink. I commented, "Can you imagine a little 1/3 horsepower garbage disposal in a $200,000 condo?" They turned around and broke into laughter. The rest of the trip, they ribbed me about my perspective of what was fun to see. (Obviously, our views were different.)

A Trust for the Future

It is important in a summer-autumn marriage to plan ahead for the eventualities of life and the certainties of death. We explored the long-range implications of the difference in our ages. We investigated the differences between wills and family trusts. We decided that it would be best to draw up a trust. During that same time period, we bought our cemetery plot.

With our retirement and move to Arizona, once again it was time to review our long term planning. It was necessary to review, revise, and rewrite our trust three times. The second time I was very uncomfortable with the manner in which it was written. Less than six months later we decided to have it reviewed by an elder law attorney. (An elder law attorney is a lawyer who specializes in laws that affect the elderly.) He found many gaps in our trust that required it to be rewritten. Under his guidance, it would be reviewed every two to three years to make certain that it was kept current with any changes in the law. We wished we had known earlier the importance of using an elder law attorney in our estate planning. In financial matters, long term planning, health care, and death issues, it is important to have specialists overseeing your plan. The peace of mind is well worth the slight difference in the cost.

As part of our long-range plan, we explored long term care insurance. We have carried a plan for about ten years. As I had the legal responsibility to handle all of Aunt Joyce's financial and health care issues, I decided to buy similar coverage for her. Due to her age, her policy could only cover a four year time period and was more expensive. It was clear - the younger one was, the better the policy coverage and the lower the premium rates were.

At seventy, health problems took over, and I slowed down. At about the same time, Sharon began having problems with fibromyalgia. We are not certain what role our exposure to stachybotrus mold spores, which attack central nervous and im-mune systems, played in our health problems. Blood tests also showed that high levels of chemicals, heavy metals, PCBs, and pesticides were in our systems. It took two years of weekly and sometimes daily visits for environmental health detoxification treatments to bring the levels down to near-tolerable levels.

Between the health issues and the need for a bio-hazard team to completely clean up our home, those two years were the most stressful to our marriage. It was further stressed with the need to dispose of all fabric-covered furnishings, replace car-peting with tile, and wipe down everything with diluted bleach water before bringing it back into our home. We faced weeks of exhaustion as we accomplished all of this. While it severely stressed us out physically, the stress drew us closer together emotionally and spiritually. We became much more protective of one another.

As with all planning, flexibility is crucial. With deteriorat-ing health, our ability to maintain our home also declined.

About four years ago, independent of each other, we were thinking about alternative living arrangements. One evening I mentioned that we should begin planning to downsize. Sharon responded that she had been thinking about the senior housing our Prescott Valley Samaritan Center planned to build. Immediately, she and I were of one mind about it! In a moment it was sealed.

> "Again I say to you that if two of you
> agree on earth concerning anything
> that they ask, it will be done for them
> by my Father in heaven." [48]

With this, as in much of our planning, various factors were involved. For several years I have been a member of the Prescott Valley Samaritan Center Advisory Board. I fully support their philosophy of ministry. It is summed up in their motto,

"In Christ's Love, everyone is someone."

I have seen this in operation throughout the organization. It is the kind of setting in which Sharon and I would be comfortable.

Another important consideration is that once we resided in one of their facilities, we would be in their continuum of care. If we came to the point of requiring additional services, we could hire outside help or move within the system to a higher level of care. In a summer-autumn marriage, this is a very important consideration. With our age difference and a history of Alzheimer's disease in Sharon's family, this would assure that a system of care is in place for her. Our trust names a loving, caring niece to handle our affairs when that becomes necessary. Even though she lives across the country, she will be able to coordinate with the facility to assure that care needs are met as they arise.

Another important consideration for us is that it gives the opportunity to develop friendships within a close-knit group. We could become isolated living alone in our home. From pastoral care experience, I know the fear of dying alone is experienced by many seniors. As chief of residential care licensing services, I saw many young families struggle with guilt and anxiety when faced with making life end decisions for their parents. Should they try to keep elderly parents in their homes, or place them in out-of-home care facilities? I firmly believe such decisions should be made by couples early in their marriages. It is important that family members know our wishes in this area. Should our families be traumatized by guilt when forced to make decisions about where we need to live because we have not made them aware of our wishes?

With all of the issues we faced, it was very clear that while we loved our home, it was time to scale-down and move to senior housing. At the next board meeting, I requested that our names be placed on the list for an apartment. We were the first couple to sign up to move into the planned apartments. Slightly more than two years later, the apartments were completed, and we were enjoying our new apartment. What a blessing it is to be sharing our lives with new found friends!

Until Death Do Us Part

One of my favorite verses of Scripture, related to aging and death, imprinted itself on my mind as I saw it unfolding in my life. The Psalmist said,

"The days of our lives are seventy years; and
if by reason of strength they are eighty years
yet their boast is only labor and sorrow; for
it is soon cut off, and we fly away." [49]

A beautiful picture comes into my mind: I see the Lord looking down upon me with a twinkle in His eye and saying,

"Don, don't say I didn't tell you—but remember how it ends."

As death is a reality and we do fly away, it became a significant part of our long-range plan. After much soul searching, we decided that cremation would be appropriate for us. This

was a difficult decision as no one in my family had ever been cremated. When I discussed it with our pastor, he said he knew of nothing in Scripture that spoke against it. This did not satisfy me. The question remained, "Is there anything in Scripture that would suggest cremation is a viable alternative to burial?"

As I reviewed Scripture more closely, I came across verses that spoke of our being created from dust and that we return to it. In Genesis 3:19, God tells Adam and Eve,

> "In the sweat of your face you shall eat bread,
> till you return to the ground; for out of it you
> were taken; for dust you are and to dust you
> shall return." [50]

> Abraham declared, in Genesis 18:27:
> "Then Abraham answered and said, "Indeed
> now, I who am but dust and ashes have
> taken upon myself to speak to the Lord:..." [51]

> In despair, Job cried out,
> "He has cast me into the mire, and I am
> become like dust and ashes," [52]

> In Ecclesiastes 12:7, the preacher proclaims,
> "Then the dust will return to the earth as it was;
> and the spirit will return to God who gave it." [53]

John, my mortician friend, defined cremation in simple terms. It is the rapid return of the body to its original state. The above verses and John's definition settled the cremation issue for us. Certainly, God created us from the dust of the earth and can raise us from that state into our spiritual bodies.

With the decision made, Sharon and I bought cremation insurance plans and sold our cemetery plot. We have arranged for our cremation with very clear guidelines regarding removing my remains and the time of my cremation.

Having worked closely with our funeral director over the

years, I have a "dark humor" understanding with him regarding how he is to remove my remains. It came about from the following incident. I was riding back from conducting a memorial service with him when the front tire blew out and did quite a bit of damage to the hearse. When it was repaired, he decided to have it repainted from black to a combination of maroon and silver. A short time later when I was admiring the new paint job, I commented that I guessed as I would be cremated, I wouldn't get a chance to ride in the back of the hearse. (Normally, they remove remains in a smaller vehicle.) He smiled and responded, "Don't worry, Don, I'll see that you get to ride in the back. We'll pick you up in this one."

I replied, "It has always been comfortable riding up front. I'm sure I won't complain about the ride in the back."

In my guidelines, I have asked whoever calls the mortuary to remind them to pick me up in the maroon and silver Cadillac. I want my last ride to be first class.

The cremation is to be on the third day following my death, symbolic of Christ's resurrection. We arranged to have our ashes buried under our markers in the Precious Memories Rose Garden at Heritage Cemetery. I facetiously told my friend at Heritage that burying them certainly beat spreading them on a windy day!

I believe as much as possible should be done in planning for one's death. It is not a morbid fixation on death, but assumption of responsibility for one's life and death issues. Every effort should be made to relieve family members of major decisions when they are facing the trauma of their loved one's death.

I recently visited a widow whose husband had a lingering illness. Just before his death, she was discussing with him his wishes concerning cremation and memorial planning. Her sixty-year-old son confronted her about talking to his dad about death issues when he was dying! She explained that they had discussed and planned for their deaths for years. She was merely confirming that it was his continuing desire to follow what they had previously planned. The son continued to have difficulty with it. Unlike the reaction of this son, it is important that

family members accept and support the realistic plans of their parents. Parents should involve their children as early as possible in the planning process.

Another area we discussed was memorial planning. In planning for my memorial service, I have outlined the Scriptures to be used, what they mean to me, have written a poem about the verses, and have indicated what hymns are to be sung. A poem to my wife, family, and friends will also be read. I gave a copy of the material to our minister and left a copy in our safe.

A final part of my plan is a step-by-step outline of contacts to be made including phone numbers and addresses. The packet contains a list of where important documents are filed. Those who will play significant roles in helping Sharon settle our trust, legal, and financial issues have been made aware of their roles. A farewell letter saying goodbye to family and friends is printed and ready for mailing. Address labels are filed with the letter.

While my experience and plan have been developed as part of the responsibility I feel toward my younger spouse, I believe it is an important factor to consider in all marriages. What greater gift can we give to our loved ones at the time of our deaths than a well laid out plan for our memorial services and for meeting their ongoing needs?

With these matters in order, Sharon and I can focus our attention on our love for each other and sharing time together. As she approaches the early winter of life and I move toward those final blustery days of winter, what joy and hope we share in our match made in Sunday school and designed in Heaven. We shout a resounding, "YES! He makes divorce and remarriage beautiful in His time!"

Two Poems

This poem was written to a co-worker and his fiancé after a discussion with him about the age difference with which they were struggling. It was much the same dilemma I faced when first starting to date Sharon. Their love has lasted into early fall and winter. Robert and Christina have been married over twenty years. They now have two college age children.

Different Seasons

She was in her mid-summer
So radiant, warm and fair.
Her smile was bright sunshine
As I saw her sitting there.

I was walking in the cooling air
Of my late Autumn days.
The frost of life's experiences
Had turned my hair to grey.

I wondered as we talked there,
Was it fair of me to date?
She was so young and beautiful,
How could our hearts relate?

She told me, oh, so gently,
"Give our love a chance to grow,
It's better we share it briefly,
Than its joys to never know."

Her words of wondrous wisdom
Brought my heart a special peace.
Now we share our love together
With all kinds of joy released.

Day by day I find love growing,
Our hearts are all aglow.
It's not the age that matters,
But how our love we show.

I know when I walk in winter,
With hair as white as snow,

She'll be standing there beside me,
Still helping me to grow.

How I love this special woman,
God has placed her in my heart.
We shall walk life's road together,
'Til by death we're torn apart.

I shall wait for her in Heaven,
As she walks her winter street.
With the Lord as her protector,
'Til in Heaven again we meet.

My friends, as you join together,
Late spring and early Fall,
May you find in love's embraces,
Seasons matter not at all.

May you walk with hearts together,
Through the seasons of your years.
May your love continue growing,
And your marriage know no fears.

Don E. Cunningham

Don E. Cunningham

He Holds My Hand

Psalm 73:23 & 24

My loved one passed beyond the vale,
My body aches—my heart doth fail.
Others go on with happy lives,
I wonder how my soul survives.

Dread sorrow holds me in its grasp
"I'm all alone," my heart doth gasp.
A numbness pounds within my head,
I can't believe my loved one's dead.

I must go on, does no one care?
I sit alone my cross to bear.
My teardrops fall like heavy rain,
It seems I'll never laugh again.

A voice within me soft but clear,
Declares, "You are my temple dear,
I am your Holy Comforter,
I dwell within—your heart to stir.

Look up in hope, I hold your hand,
I came to help you understand,
Christ came to die, His life to give,
So that you may forever live.

You walk the valley in this life,
Know heartache, sorrow, pain and strife.
Come friend I hold you by the hand,
I'll guide you on to glory land!"

With faith move on—be patient, friend,
You'll meet your loved one at trail's end.

Live on in hope—do not despair,
Eternal life awaits you there!

In Christ's Love,

Don Cunningham
6/27/99

Help Along Your Way – Questions For Reflection

1. What marital adjustments are included in your retirement planning?

2. What are important factors in developing a long term plan for your future?

3. Name the advantages, even when young and healthy, of involving an elder lawyer in developing a Family Trust?

4. Why is it important for spouses to discuss their plans for coping with health and death issues?

5. What still needs to be discussed with your spouse and family members?

Sharon's Comments: Even Truer Today

Dearest Wonderful Husband

It seems so hard to believe we've had two years of marriage already. I want to savor our time together, so I hate to see it flow so quickly. I remember writing you a letter on our last anniversary and thought it might be nice to do again. I remember listing the worries and concerns I had to overcome when we got married. Funny, you know I don't recall what they were. All my memories are of the contented moments of this past year—moments spent at your side or in your arms.

I bask in your love and the wonderful way you accept me with all my shortcomings and eccentricities (even pretending I don't have any). How can I tell you how much I love and appreciate you? That beyond my loving you as I do, I see you as a man to admire, be proud of, respect . . . whose value is "far above rubies." Of course it is possible I may be highly prejudiced, but I believe I married one of God's finest.

I know many people get married with "stars in their eyes" and then reality sets in and the glow wears off. I know usually couples have to undergo a "period of adjustment." Why haven't we experienced this? I guess the Lord just matched us so well that we didn't need it. I do know I love you even more than on our first anniversary or even our honeymoon. Sometime I still have trouble believing how beautiful our marriage is. I remember your telling me about your list of "what you wanted in a wife." Have I ever told you that I didn't even know what a good husband was like? I didn't know enough to even make a list. But God has shown me, through you, what His list is like, and I love the example.

We have had a good full year this last year—blest with each other's love, good health, good friends, material goods, and even travel "adventure"! How good God has been to us! My cup truly "runneth over."

I don't know what the Lord has in store for us this next

year. It has to be for good. As we are told, we'll just have to trust, won't we? I am not so afraid of losing any of my earthly possessions (I've been poor before). I only pray we never lose our love for each other. All the "things" in my life could be gone tomorrow, and as long as you were with me, it would be bearable. On the other hand, if you weren't at my side, the "things" wouldn't mean a thing!

Wonderful husband; my friend, my lover; half of "my flesh"; please forgive my not always being alert to your needs and not always being the wife I'd like to be. You never make me feel I've let you down, yet I know there must be times . . .

I love you so very, very much. Thank you for another wonderful year of being your wife.

~Sharon

It has been twenty-five years since I wrote this letter to Don. As you can tell from what he has written in previous chapters, we have had many challenges to our marriage. These outside forces and health problems have only strengthened our marriage. During the ensuing years, the things I said in my letter have deepened in meaning. We have parted with many of our earthly possessions. We have gone from owning a lovely home to renting a much smaller apartment. The ravages of mold, chemicals, pesticides, etc., have compromised our immune and central nervous systems. Other major health conditions have taken their toll upon us.

Yes, things and health have disappeared, but we are still husband and wife, friends and lovers. While our flesh is no longer as strong as it used to be, we are still one flesh in Christ. It seems like the older and weaker we become, the closer we are bound together in love. It is my sincere prayer that those who read this book may experience the joy and love Don and I have shared. We can tell you from experience that Christ and His Word truly can make divorce and remarriage beautiful in His time.

~Sharon Cunningham

Don and Sharon celebrating their twenty-fifth wedding anniversary at the Peacock Room

Appendix A

The poem written below, with applicable verses interspersed between stanzas, may help you experience the richness of God's Word as you apply it throughout your journey through the valley of the shadow of divorce.

Divorce's Depression – Forgiveness's Delight

I wept all night, depressed alone,
For my sins He could not atone.
My heart broken, I wept and wept,
My soul by Him could not be kept.

Stanza One - Psalm 119:145-149 - "I cry out with my whole heart; hear me, O Lord! I will keep Your statutes. I cry out to You; Save me, and I will keep Your testimonies. I rise before the dawning of the morning, and cry for help; I hope in Your word. My eyes are awake through the night watches, that I may meditate on Your word. Hear my voice according to Your loving-kindness; O Lord, revive me according to Your justice."

I wept all night, depressed alone,
There were those who cast a first stone.
My heart cried out, "Where are you God,
Would I be best beneath the sod?"

Stanza Two - John 8:7, 10 & 11 - "So when they continued asking Him, He raised Himself up and said to them, "He who is without sin among you, let him throw a stone at her first." When

Jesus had raised Himself up and saw no one but the woman, He said to her, "Woman, where are those accusers of yours? Has no one condemned you?" She said, "No one Lord." And Jesus said to her, "Neither do I condemn you; go and sin no more."

Romans 7:24 & 25 - In chapter seven Paul struggles with the effect of the law, sin and death finally crying out, "O wretched man that I am! Who will deliver me from this body of death? I thank God—through Jesus Christ our Lord! So then, with the mind I myself serve the law of God, but with the flesh the law of sin."

Dreadful sin, in my deep remorse,
Could not keep it from its course.
Must I forever then remain,
Beneath its sinful rotten stain?

Stanza Three - Isaiah 53:5 – "But He was wounded for our transgressions, He was bruised for our iniquities; the chastisement for our peace was upon Him, and by His stripes we are healed."

I Peter 2:24 -"Who Himself bore our sins in His own body on the tree, that we, having died to sins, might live for righteousness – by whose stripes we are healed."

Hebrews 8:12 - "For I will be merciful to their unrighteousness, and their sins and their lawless deeds I will remember no more."

Then one bright night a new song came,
It did my raging heartache tame.
It sang of broken hearts and plans,
And said to place them in Christ's hands.

Stanza 4 - Doug Oldham sang the hymn "Pick Up The Broken Pieces." This hymn speaks of failing and not accomplishing what you wanted to in your life. It goes on to tell you to pick up the pieces and take them to our understanding Savior.

It gave me the picture of my broken platter of life needing to be cleansed and put back together by our Lord.

> Divorce is a sin composite,
> My heart doth grieve and wants to quit.
> In hardened arteries of my soul,
> I let sins take their dreadful toll.

Stanza Five - Matthew 5:4 - "Blessed are those who mourn, for they shall be comforted."

Romans 8:16 - "The Spirit Himself bears witness with our spirit that we are the children of God."

> A hardened heart, shattered, broken,
> The Potter's hand it has spoken.
> Pick up each piece as it's my sin
> Let my Lord cleanse me from within.

Stanza Six - Psalm 95-7b&8a - "Today, if you will hear His voice; do not harden your hearts, as in the rebellion."

Isaiah 64:8 - "But now, O Lord, You are our Father; We are the clay, and You our potter; and all we are the works of Your Hand."

Romans 9:21-23 - "Does not the potter have power over the clay, from the same lump to make one vessel for honor and another for dishonor? What if God, wanting to show His wrath and to make His power known, endured with much long-suffering the vessels of wrath prepared for destruction, and that He might make known the riches of His glory on the vessels of mercy, which He had prepared beforehand for His glory, even us whom He called not of the Jews only, but also of the gentiles?"

> Then I came to my Savior fair,
> Confessed each sin and tarried there.
> He cleansed me of my sins galore,

And told me, "Go, and sin no more."

Stanza Seven—Same verses as Stanza 2—John 8:7-10 & 11.

I John 1:9 - "If we confess our sins, He is faithful and just to forgive us our sins and to cleanse us from all unrighteousness."

My spirit leapt, I found His grace,
Each of my sins was cleansed—erased.
I could rejoice in heart and soul.
You see, His grace had made me whole.

Stanza Eight - Ephesians 2:8-10 - "For by grace you have been saved through faith, and that not of yourselves; it is the grace of God, not of works, lest anyone should boast. For we are His workmanship, created in Christ Jesus for good works, which God prepared beforehand that we should walk in them."

Fresh tears flowed down, I found release
My Savior brought me precious peace.
A special text, I now make mine,
'Tis First John one, the verse is nine.

Stanza Nine - I John 1:9 - Same as stanza seven I John 1:9

Now free at last my loss was gain,
As His blessed child I still remain.
Dear Lord don't ever let me slip,
And lose our precious fellowship.

Stanza Ten - John 1:12 - "But as many as received Him, to them He gave the right to become children of God, to those who believe in His name."

Romans 8:14–16 - "For as many as are led by the Spirit of God, these are sons of God. For you did not receive the spirit of bondage again to fear but you received the Spirit of adoption

by whom we cry out, 'Abba, Father.' The Spirit Himself bears witness with our spirit that we are the children of God."

Philippians 2:1 & 2 - "Therefore if there is any consolation in Christ, if any comfort of love, if any fellowship of the Spirit, if any affection and mercy, fulfill my joy by being like-minded, having the same love, being of one accord, of one mind."

II Corinthians 13:14 - "The grace of the Lord Jesus Christ, and the love of God, and the communion of the Holy Spirit be with you all. Amen."

Appendix B

A Short Story

While reflecting on my growth experiences related in Chapter VIII, I decided to write a short story of how the verses in Leviticus, cited in the chapter, might work out in Old Testament times. I hope you will find it helpful in relating your divorce experience to your relationship with our Lord and His church. Be assured He wants to share His table with you!

MARA (Bitterness, Sorrow)

Tears flowed from her swollen red eyes as she sat on a mound of dirt alongside the road just outside the Damascus gate. Her body shook and ribs ached as she sat weeping. A dark cloud of bitterness swept through her as she stared at the wrinkled, tear-stained scroll in her hand. That morning, her husband had denounced her and signed the writing of divorcement, known as a "get," in the presence of those self-righteous witnesses and the rabbi seated at the city gate. He cast her out of his house as an obnoxious wife. She had been unable to bear him any children. This little scroll showed that the get was on file with the rabbi. It was the final devastating blow to her childhood dream of being the perfect wife and mother.

Her father had warned her not to marry outside of the priesthood of Israel. He had quoted the law to her. After all, was she not the daughter of a priest of the Holy God who had given His law to guide His children into all holiness? She was in love, and what did her father know about love? She kicked the dirt beneath her feet. If only she had listened to her father, Ellebab (Heart of God). If only he had been more firm. If only . . .

Tears of bitterness and anxiety flowed down her cheeks and fell in droplets at her feet. Where could she turn now? Her parents had named her well, for Mara was drinking of the cup of bitterness. She was a marked woman, stained by the sin of divorce—an outcast woman!

Darkness fell quickly over the city as ever-darkening fears began to take over the deepest recesses of Mara's mind. The chill of the night settled in around her. Slowly she lifted her ex-hausted body up from the dirt pile and trudged wearily through the city gate. Where could she turn now? To whom could she turn? Surely she could not return to her father's house. Every-thing seemed so hopeless. Was life even worth living? Oh, if only she could die.

She wandered aimlessly through the dark, narrow streets. Every little shadowy movement in doorways wrought new fears in her heart. She passed gaudily dressed, brazen women of the street. Was this to become her lot in life? How else could she survive? She had no skills with which to make a living. Her focus of life until now had been to be a housewife and to raise a family. Had this goal in life now become her downfall? Had she only been able to give her husband a boy child, how different her life might be. Again, the "if onlys" began to flow through her mind. "If only" was not going to give her a place to sleep tonight or put food in her mouth. She need not worry about food on her table; she had no table. She leaned against a wall and slowly sank to the pavement. Tonight the street would be her fear-ridden sleeping place. She fell wearily into a restless sleep. A drunken street beggar tripped over Mara, awaking her with a start. She screamed out! He cursed her for tripping him up and staggered off. Mara felt the chill of the night and began to shiver. Slowly she got up, shook the dirt from her clothing, and wandered down the dark, lonely streets. Finally, exhausted, she huddled in a doorway and sobbed herself to sleep. Tomor-row would be a new day.

Early the next morning, she was awakened by the sound of

a donkey cart bouncing over the cobblestone streets. Jerusalem was coming back to life. Mara stood up, shook the dirt off her skirt, and walked to the market area. She went from little vegetable stands, to fruit stands, to meat markets, looking for work. It was all to no avail. Her stomach ached for food. She saw an apple in the gutter, picked it up, wiped it on her skirt, and ate it. All day long she wandered from shop to shop. There was no work for her.

Once again, night began to fall over Jerusalem. Mara looked for a place to sleep. She sobbed softly as she plodded wearily along the darkened streets. As she turned a corner, there before her stood a gaily-dressed, heavily made-up, perfumed prostitute plying her trade with a young man. Mara watched as they walked toward a house and disappeared through the open doorway. The door closed behind them.

She began to think perhaps she, too, should become a prostitute. At least she would have food, a warm place to sleep, and pretty clothing. After all, no one loved her. Being barren, what man would want to marry her? Had not her husband abused and discarded her into the street like garbage? Certainly no man could treat her worse. What did she have to lose?

She struggled with the thought throughout the evening. Finally, she vowed she would not forsake the training of her childhood. She would remain faithful to her God. Prostitution would not be her lot in life. She would starve first! A new peace settled over her. Huddled in a doorway, she fell asleep.

A barking dog awakened Mara with a start. As her fright slowly disappeared, she felt a gnawing in her stomach. How hungry she was. She brushed herself off and headed for the market place. Once again she made her weary trek through the market place to look for work. She ate discarded, rotten fruits and vegetable. A discard eating discards.

Every time she approached a shopkeeper for work and was told, "Sorry, I don't need any help," she became more and more disheartened. Slowly she wandered down the last street in the market area. At the end of the street, she saw a kosher poultry market. She watched as they killed and plucked the chickens.

She went inside and hesitantly asked the young owner, Rabbi David (beloved), if she could work there. To her amazement he told her she could help his wife, Naomi (blessed), pluck the chickens. He handed her an apron and told her to watch Naomi as she plucked the birds. His was a kosher shop, and everything had to be done in a prescribed manner. He took a chicken and hung its feet through a metal loop. He then slit its neck from the front to the back. Immediately his wife started plucking. Mara watched as the blood and feathers blended together upon the stone floor. Now it was her turn to pluck the dangling birds. She hesitated, then dug her fingers into the feathers and began to pull them out. Blood splattered her apron as she plucked the feathers from the dangling, dying chicken. When she finished, Rabbi David completed the soaking, salting, and rinsing. In accord with kosher ritual, he gave it a final inspection before approving it for sale.

Finally, the long day over, Mara removed her apron and wearily walked toward the door. Naomi asked her where she lived.

Hesitantly she responded, "Here in Jerusalem."

"I know, but where do you eat and sleep?" she asked.

Mara despondently replied, "On the street."

"No!" interjected David, who had been listening to their conversation. "We have a little room at the back of our market. You can sleep there and eat here with us."

A faint smile crossed Mara's face as she realized they cared for and accepted her.

Naomi placed her arm around Mara and said, "Come, I'll show you your room."

Mara collapsed into her arms and began to cry. Her emotions, finally released, came out in uncontrollable sobs. Naomi quietly comforted her as she led her to her room. What a blessed and loving couple they were.

For the first time since her writing of divorcement, Mara slept securely and soundly. She awoke to the soft voice of Naomi calling her to come and share breakfast with her and David.

She hesitated at first, but when David insisted, she knew they sincerely wanted her to join them.

As the day and work wore on, her fingers began to ache from plucking the chickens. She was surprised at how tiring the work was. With the encouragement she was receiving from Naomi and David, she knew she would adjust to her new job and begin to find a new direction in her life.

The days turned into weeks, and Mara was slowly adjusting to her new way of life. The skin on her hands toughened and was no longer raw at the end of a day's work. David and Naomi had become like a brother and sister to her, but at night she found herself wishing that she could see her mother and father. If only they could understand and accept her. She was too embarrassed to go up to the temple area to see them.

Ellebab's heart had broken when his daughter, Mara, belligerently ignored his pleas for her to not marry outside the priesthood. She told him she was in love, and what did he know about love? Now, five years later, his heart was wrenched again as rumors drifted from the Damascus gate that Mara's husband had given her a writing of divorcement and cast her out of his house. How she must be hurting. What would happen to her now? How would she feed and clothe herself? Would she go her own way, perhaps even give her body for bread and drink? Oh, Mara, Mara, if you had only listened, how different things might be.

Ellebab tossed and turned night after night, worrying what might be happening to his precious Mara. What was happening to her? Where was she? What would she do now? If only he had been more firm with her. If only she knew how much he loved her. The scar on his heart, etched by her words, "Father, what do you know about love?" seemed to open and fester again. Oh, if only she knew how much he loved her. He must find her, reassure her of his love, and bring her back home with him.

Week after week, he prayed for his little Mara. One day as he was walking through the streets of Jerusalem, looking for her, he met a fellow priest whom he hadn't seen for quite some time. They greeted one another. As they talked, Ellebab began to unburden himself about his concern for his poor little Mara. To his surprise, the priest told him he saw a young woman who looked somewhat like her working in a small poultry market on the outskirts of town. Ellebab's heart leapt within him. Could it be his Mara?

He said goodbye to his friend and scurried down the narrow streets toward the marketplace. He ran from shop to shop and finally saw a sign, "David's Kosher Poultry Market." Surely it was where his Mara was working.

With his heart beating loudly, he rushed over to the counter and asked excitedly,

"Where is my daughter?"

David looked at this bearded, red-faced man dressed in the robes of a priest and said, "No daughter of a rabbi works here."

"But she must be here. A friend told me a young woman who looked like her was working here," Ellebab replied.

"We only have one person working here with us; a frail, sickly young woman named Mara," David responded.

"Mara, my Mara," Ellebab burst forth. "Where is she?"

"She's out back, through that door."

Scarcely had the words left David's lips when Ellebab bolted past him and through the door. There he saw his blood-splattered, chicken-feathered daughter. "Mara!" he cried. He threw his arms around her, hugged and kissed her. Mara was shocked it was her father! She had not felt that rugged reassuring hug since she was a little girl.

A thought jolted her mind: "How could her father forgive her after she brought such shame upon his name?" He had warned her that she should not marry this outsider. Her marriage would not work out. His prediction had come true. She was divorced. Yet how wonderful it was to feel his strong arms around her.

Then she heard his soft, muffled sob and felt his warm tears running down the side of her face. His body shook as the sobs increased. She had never seen her father cry before. How she

had hurt him! She burst into tears as she tried to ask for his for-giveness. "I am sorry, so sorry, father," she sobbed.

"It is all right, Mara. Please come home with me. Your mother and I have missed you so," he replied.

"But, but father, I am a divorced woman. I have brought shame upon your name. How can you and God forgive me?" cried Mara.

"We already have. Our love for you has not changed," replied Ellebab.

"Come now, come home with me. Tonight, we shall cel-ebrate. We shall eat my portion of the peace offering as a fam-ily," Ellebab said with joy.

How well Mara remembered the peace offering meals she had enjoyed with her family when she was growing up. It had been five long years since she had partaken of it. How the joy began to well up in her heart as she thought about returning home to her father's house. But how could she bring further shame upon her father and blaspheme God by eating food from His altar? She sadly looked at her father and said, "Dear father, how much I would love to do that, but I cannot return home and embarrass you further. I have sinned against God and you. I will not put you through further shame. I have failed you and God."

"You have shamed neither God nor me. He has declared you clean and fit to eat at my table. So come home with me. It shall be as it was. We shall rejoice together in the presence of Jehovah! Have you forgotten that the Peace offering is a free-will sacrifice upon the burnt sacrifice? Our sins are forgiven and we fellowship in peace. Not only I, but God has invited you home," Ellebab replied joyously.

Slowly, Mara turned to her friends, Rabbi David and Nao-mi. "What shall I do?" she asked. "You have been so good to me."

Sensing her love for her father and desire to return to her father's house, Naomi responded, "Mara, we love you and will miss you, but your place is in your father's house and at his table."

Mara returned to her home. It was as it had been. She feasted together with her family; breaking unleavened bread and eating of the meat of the peace offering. How she savored it—the taste of love and forgiveness!

Appendix C

The following poem with verses of applicable Scripture interspersed between each stanza may help one understand that God's Word is there to help us as we grow through our often-times lonely journey of divorce.

Divorce and God's Grace

For months I struggle—really grope,
A divorced person without hope.
My world exploded—blown apart,
My sins have broken my hard heart.

Stanza 1 – Mark 10:2-5 – The Pharisees came and asked Him, "Is it lawful for a man to divorce his wife?" testing Him. And He answered and said to them, "What did Moses command you?" They said, "Moses permitted a man to write a certificate of divorce, and to dismiss her." And Jesus answered and said to them, "Because of the hardness of your heart he wrote you this precept."

Friends departed, I am alone,
Even God's grace cannot atone.
Divorce has come through my cold heart,
My sins keep me and God apart

Stanza 2 – Psalm 38:11 – "My loved ones and my friends stand aloof from my plague, and my relatives stand afar off."
Psalm 142:4 – "Look on my right hand and see, for there

is no one who acknowledges me; Refuge has failed me; No one cares for my soul."

Psalm 40:12 – "For innumerable evils have surrounded me, my iniquities have overtaken me, so that I am not able to look up; they are more than the hairs of my head; therefore my heart fails me."

If divorce is beyond God's grace,
I must run a grief-stricken race.
My heart and soul are in despair,
Can it be that God does not care?

Stanza 3 – I Peter 5:7 – "Casting all your care upon Him, for He cares for you."

He says he heals the broken heart,
And gives us all a fresh new start,
And yet I hear preachers proclaim,
"You, the divorced, must bear your shame!"

Stanza 4 – Psalm 34:18 – "The Lord is near to those who have a broken heart, and saves such as have a contrite spirit."
Ps. 51:17 – "Purge me with hyssop, and I shall be clean; wash me, and I shall be whiter than snow."

Mind and soul confused, in distress,
Who will save me from my mess?
God forgives murderer and thief,
Yet His grace cannot spare my grief.

Stanza 5 – Matthew 27:44 – "Even the robbers who were crucified with Him reviled Him with the same thing.
Luke 23:39 – 43 – Then one of the criminals who were hanged blasphemed Him, saying, 'If You are the Christ save Yourself and us.' But the other, answering, rebuked him, saying, 'Do you not even fear God, seeing you are under the same condemnation?' "And we indeed justly, for we receive the due

reward of our deeds; but this Man has done nothing wrong." Then he said to Jesus, "Lord, remember me when You come into Your kingdom." And Jesus said to him, "Assuredly, I say to you, today, you will be with Me in Paradise."

Can it be that my God is dead?
In his Word, this I never read.
His Spirit's Love touches my heart,
"I still love you, we'll never part."

Stanza 6 – John 14:16 – 18 – "And I will pray the Father and He will give you another Helper, that He may abide with you forever-the Spirit of truth, whom the world cannot receive, because it neither sees Him nor knows Him; but you know Him, for He dwells with you and will be in you. I will not leave you orphans; I will come to you."

Hebrews 13:5 & 6 – "Let your conduct be without covetousness; be content with such things as you have. For He Himself has said, 'I will never leave you nor forsake you.' So we may boldly say, "The Lord is my helper; I will not fear. What can man do to me?"

Death of a marriage His voice still heard,
"Child, please study my precious Word.
In Scriptures my truth is revealed,
Study its pages and be healed."

Stanza 7 – II Timothy 2:15 – "Be diligent to present yourself approved to God, a worker who does not need to be ashamed, rightly dividing the word of truth."

II Timothy 3:16 & 17 – "All Scripture is given by inspiration of God, and is profitable for doctrine, for reproof, for correction for instruction in righteousness, that the man of God may be complete, thoroughly equipped for every good work."

I studied its pages and found,
Sin abounded, grace more abounds.

Does it work with sins of divorce?
Can it be He shares my remorse?

Stanza 8 – Romans 5:19 & 20 – "For as by one man's dis-
obedience many were made sinners, so also by one Man's obedience many will be made righteous. Moreover the law entered
that the offense might abound. But where sin abounded, grace
abounded much more."
Isaiah 53:12 – "He shall see the labor of His soul, and be
satisfied. By His knowledge My righteous Servant shall justify
many."

I look in His law, find His grace,
Great tears of joy flow down my face.
Divorced daughter at table eats,
Sits with priest father, shares his meats!

Stanza 9 – Leviticus 22:13 – "But if the priest's daughter is
a widow or divorced, and has no child, and has returned to her
father's house as in her youth, she may eat her father's food; but
no outsider shall eat it."

Christ never divorced. Can it be,
He was tempted and tried like me?
Look to the prophets in remorse.
Their words show God got a divorce!

Stanza 10 – Hebrews 4:14 & 15 – "Seeing then that we
have a great High Priest who has passed through the heavens,
Jesus the Son of God, let us hold fast our confession. For we do
not have a High Priest who cannot sympathize with our weaknesses, but was in all points tempted as we are, yet without
sin."
Jeremiah 3:8 – "Then I saw that for all the causes for which
backsliding Israel had committed adultery, I had put her away
and given her a certificate of divorce; yet her treacherous sister
Judah did not fear, but went and played the harlot also."

Christ gave his body for me and you
Sins forgiven through His blood, too.
Man of sorrows, stricken with grief,
Brings me forgiveness—sweet relief!

Stanza 11 – Matthew 26:26 – 28 – "And as they were eating, Jesus took bread, blessed and broke it, and gave it to the disciples and said, 'Take, eat; this is My body.' Then He took the cup and gave thanks, and gave it to them, saying, 'Drink from it, all of you. For this is My blood of the new covenant, which is shed for many for the remission of sins'."

Isaiah 53:3 – "He is despised and rejected by men, A Man of sorrows and acquainted with grief. And we hid, as it were, our faces from Him; He was despised, and we did not esteem Him."

Yes, a hardened heart has been healed,
As it was broken, sins revealed.
Christ helped me see them—I confessed,
Then He forgave me, cleansed and blessed.

Stanza 12 – I John 1:9 - "If we confess our sins, He is faithful and just to forgive us our sins and to cleanse us from all unrighteousness."

SELECTED BIBLIOGRAPHY

Allison, Susan. *Conscious Divorce*, Three Rivers Press, (Crown Publishing Co.) 2001

Campolo, Tony. *The Kingdom of God Is A Party*, Word Publishing

Ellison, Stanley A. *Divorce And Remarriage In The Church*, The Zondervan Corp, 1977

Hetherington, E. Mavie & Kelly, John. *For Better Or For Worse: Divorce Reconsidered*,W.W. Norton & Company, Inc.2002

Hickey, Elizabeth, MSW & Dalton, Elizabeth, JD. *Healing Hearts (Helping Children and Adults Recover from Divorce)* Gold Leaf Press, 1994

McDill, Dr. Samuel R. & McDill, Dr. S. Rutherford, Jr., *The Master's Design For Discovering Your Self*, Self Published, 1985, Library of Congress #203-678

Rosenstock, Harvey A. MD & Rosenstock, Judith D, PhD. *Journey Through Divorce (Five Stages Toward Recovery)*, Human Sciences Press, Inc. 1988

Silverman, Robin L., *The Ten Gifts*, St. Martin's Press, 2000

Small, Dr. Dwight. *Remarriage and God's Renewing Grace*. Baker Books, 1986

Smoke, Jim. *Growing Through Divorce*, Harvest House Publishers, 1995

Smoke, Jim. *Growing In Remarriage*, Fleming Revell, 1990

Spinnanger, Ruthe T., *Better Than Divorce*, Logos International, 1978

Steele, Paul E. & Ryrie, Charles C. *Meant to Last*, SP Publications, Inc. 1983

Wegscheider-Cruse, Sharon. *Life After Divorce (Create a New Beginning)* Health Communications, Inc. 1994

Young, Amy Ross. *By Death or Divorce. . . it hurts to lose*, Accents Publications, 1978

Zodhiates, Spiros, TH.D. *What About Divorce*. AMG Publishers, 1984

Commentaries

Barnes' *Notes On the Old & New Testament The Bible Commentary*, F.C. Cook, Editor, Exodus through Ruth, Baker Book House, Grand Rapids, Michigan

Kellogg, Rev. S.H. Kellogg, *The Expositor's Bible* Editor W. Robertson Nicoll, DD, LLD, Hodder & Stoughton, New York, NY

Lange, John Peter, *Commentary On The Holy Scriptures* Zondervan Publishing House. Grand Rapids, Michigan

McGee, J. Vernon, *Leviticus, Volumes I & II Through The Bible Books*, publisher. Pasadena, CA

Endnotes

1. Paul E. Steele & Charles C. Ryrie, *Meant to Last*, Victor Books, Wheaton, IL P. 99 - 117

2. Dr. Samuel R. McDill, Doctorate of Marriage & Family Counseling from Fuller Theological Seminary and Co-Author with his son, S. Rutherford McDill, Jr., PhD of *The Master's Design for Discovering Your Self* 1985, Library of Congress #203-678

3. Enright, Elizabeth, "A House Divided" Article in AARP Magazine, July-August, 2004.

4. Montenegro, Xenia P., PhD. "The Divorce Experience-A Study of Divorce at Midlife and Beyond" Survey conducted by Knowledge Networks, Inc. for AARP The Magazine (On their website – www.aarp.org)

5. Mark 16:14 NKJV

6. Darlene Petri, *The Hurt and Healing of Divorce*, David C. Cook, Publishing Co., p. 116

7. Philippians 4:4 NKJV

8. Numbers 30:9-11 NKJV

9. Galatians 6:2-5 NKJV

10. Psalm 62:1 and 68:20 NKJV

11. James 3:6 NKJV

12. James 1:26 NKJV

13. Tony Campolo, *The Kingdom of God Is A Party*, Word Publishing, Dallas, TX 1990, 150 pages.

14. I John 1:8-10 – NKJV

15. Ephesians 4:26 NKJV

16. Matthew 18:22 NKJV

17. Matthew 6:12 NKJV

18. Psalm 119:163 NKJV

19. Proverbs 13.5 NKJV

20. Romans 1:28-30 NKJV

21. James 1:26 NKJV

22. James 3:8b-10 NKJV

23. John 20:22b-23 NKJV

24. Leviticus 22:13 NKJV

25. Kellogg, DD, Rev. S.H., *The Expositor's Bible*, p.98. Hodder & Stoughton Publishers

26. Barnes', *Notes On The Old And New Testaments - The Bible Commentary*, Exodus – Ruth, Baker Book House, p. 116 footnote.

27. McGee, J. Vernon, *Leviticus Volumes I* (p. 32) *& II* (p, 269), Through the Bible Books Publisher.

28. Leviticus 7:12 & 13 NKJV

29. Lange, John Peter, *Commentary On The Holy Scriptures* p. 86, Zondervan Publishing House, Grand Rapids, Michigan.

30. Leviticus 7:19 & 20 NJKV

31. Leviticus 22:3 NKJV

32. I Corinthians 11:28 & 29 NKJV

33. I John 1:9 NKJV

34. Hebrews 4:15 NKJV

35. Jeremiah 3:8 NKJV

36. Jeremiah 2:13 NJKV

37. Jeremiah 3:1 NJKV

38. Strong, Augustus F., *Systematic Theology*, p.1035, Judson Press, Philadelphia, PA

39. Romans 12:15 NKJV

40. John 11:35 NKJV

41. Ephesians 4:31 – 32 NKJV

42. Matthew 19:3 – 9 NKJV

43. Matthew 19:10 – 12 NKJV

44. Genesis 2:18 NKJV

45. Eric Berne, Psychiatrist was the founder of "Transactional Analysis". He refers to "Ego states" as Child, Adult and Parent. Therapy includes analysis of the transaction levels during conversations between individuals. It involves life scripts, games people play, giving people strokes, I'm OK – You're OK and contracts to resolve issues.

46. I Timothy 3:2 & 12 NKJV.

47. Jim Smoke, *Growing In Remarriage*, Fleming H. Revell Co., 1990, pgs 119-125.

48. Matthew 18:19 NKJV

49. Psalm 90:10 NKJV

50. Genesis 3:19 NKJV

51. Genesis 18:27 NKJV

52. Job 30:19 NKJV

53. Ecclesiastes 12:7 NKJV

T A T E P U B L I S H I N G *&* *Enterprises*

Tate Publishing is commited to excellence in the publishing industry. Our staff of highly trained professionals, including editors, graphic designers, and marketing personnel, work together to produce the very finest books available. The company reflects the philosophy established by the founders, based on Psalms 68:11,

"THE LORD GAVE THE WORD AND GREAT WAS THE COMPANY OF THOSE WHO PUBLISHED IT."

If you would like further information, please call
1.888.361.9473
or visit our website
www.tatepublishing.com

T A T E P U B L I S H I N G *&* *Enterprises*, LLC
127 E. Trade Center Terrace
Mustang, Oklahoma 73064 USA